Shakespeare & Stratford

Shakespeare &

Series Editors:
Graham Holderness, *University of Hertfordshire*
Bryan Loughrey

Shakespeare & Stratford

Edited by
Katherine Scheil

berghahn
NEW YORK · OXFORD
www.berghahnbooks.com

Published in 2019 by
Berghahn Books
www.berghahnbooks.com

© 2019 Berghahn Books

Originally published as a special issue
of *Critical Survey*, volume 24, number 2.

Library of Congress Cataloging-in-Publication Data

Names: Scheil, Katherine West, 1966– editor.
Title: Shakespeare and Stratford / edited by Katherine Scheil.
Description: New York : Berghahn Books, 2019. | Series: Shakespeare and ;
    volume 1 | Includes bibliographical references and index.
Identifiers: LCCN 2019008160 (print) | LCCN 2019010937 (ebook) | ISBN
    9781789202571 (ebook) | ISBN 9781789202557 (hardback : alk. paper) |
    ISBN 9781789202564(paperback : alk. paper)
Subjects: LCSH: Shakespeare, William, 1564–1616—Homes and
    haunts—England—Stratford-upon-Avon. | Dramatists, English—Homes
    and haunts—England—Stratford-upon-Avon. | Stratford-upon-Avon
    (England)—In literature.
Classification: LCC PR2916 (ebook) | LCC PR2916 .S15 2019 (print) | DDC
    822.3/3—dc23
LC record available at https://lccn.loc.gov/2019008160

British Library Cataloguing in Publication Data

A catalogue record for this book is available from the British Library

ISBN 978-1-78920-255-7 hardback
ISBN 978-1-78920-256-4 paperback
ISBN 978-1-78920-257-1 ebook

This book is dedicated with love to
Christy Desmet (1954–2018):
Shakespeare and Stratford
held a special place in her heart.

Contents

Illustrations

Preface

Katherine Scheil

According to actor Nick Asbury, Stratford-upon-Avon is 'a wonderful, strange, old place ... a place of dreams'.[1] As the site of literary pilgrimage since the eighteenth century, the home of the Royal Shakespeare Company and the topic of hundreds of imaginary portrayals, Stratford is ripe for analysis, both in terms of its factual existence and its fictional afterlife. The chapters in this volume consider the various manifestations of the physical and metaphorical town on the Avon, across time, genre and place, from America to New Zealand, from children's literature to wartime commemorations. We meet many Stratfords in this collection, real and imaginary, and the interplay between the two generates new visions of the place. The chapters in this collection, summarised in Nicola Watson's afterword, begin to write a history of these imagined Stratfords.

Every reimagining of Stratford assembles a combination of real locales such as Holy Trinity Church, the Henley Street Birthplace, Anne Hathaway's Cottage and New Place, and adds a notion of 'Shakespeare' to produce a particular conception of 'Stratford'. These

Notes for this section begin on page 3.

various town landmarks also reveal their own narratives of Stratford. A fixture in Stratford since 1210, Holy Trinity Church has inspired scholars as well as tourists, relic hunters and would-be grave robbers. As Clara Calvo writes in her chapter for this collection, even a single window in Holy Trinity Church (the American Memorial Window) can have its own 'cultural biography' (60) connecting Shakespeare, Stratford and international relations. The changing physical spaces of the geographical Stratford, such as the excavation of Shakespeare's last home New Place and the re-opening of the Shakespeare Memorial Theatre, provide fodder for what Nicola Watson calls in her afterword 'recognisably new stories' (95) waiting to be told.

Imaginative portrayals of Stratford comprise a significant portion of material on Stratford. From the young adult fiction that Susanne Greenhalgh covers in her chapter to detective novels, conceptions of Stratford resonate outside its geographical and temporal boundaries, disseminating ideas of Englishness and 'Shakespeare country' well beyond the local community. Katherine Scheil's contribution to this collection traces the various places around the world that have sought to call 'Stratford' home, in New Zealand and New Jersey alike.

In addition to the thousands of tourists who visit year-round, various other pilgrims have left their marks on Stratford, reshaping the space for various personal and public purposes. Stratford has a long tradition as an actor's town, from travelling players who visited during Shakespeare's lifetime, through contemporary actors with the Royal Shakespeare Company. Many of these actors have had a major role in shaping the later history of Stratford. Actor Thomas Betterton was the first to research the details of Shakespeare's life for Nicholas Rowe's seminal 1709 biography, and actor David Garrick inaugurated the Stratford tourist trade with his 1769 Shakespeare Jubilee. Christy Desmet's chapter on Helen Faucit traces the town through one actress's experience, looking at the junction between 'what Helen Faucit meant to Stratford and what the Stratford experience meant to her' (4).

The history of Stratford has been told by historians, archaeologists, Bardolators and anti-Bardolators alike, and through individuals or collectively through groups. Stratford might also be analysed through different modes of perception – through walking tours (as Julie Sanders shows in her chapter), tourist experiences and armchair travellers. 'Stratford' can even exist outside Warwickshire – in

New Zealand, Canada and America.[2] Future work might explore the collective experience of tourist groups who visit the Stratford properties, as well as the experiences of various national groups.[3]

Even anti-Stratfordians have not been immune to this 'wonderful strange old place'. American anti-Stratfordian Delia Bacon made the 'last expedition of her life' to Stratford, where she planned to open the tomb of Shakespeare and discover papers revealing the real authorship of the plays.[4] Bacon wrote in 1856, 'I love to be here. Those beautiful trees and that church spire look a little like dreamland to me'.[5] The many reconstructions of the 'dream-land' of 'Stratford' in literature, art and around the globe suggest that ideas of Stratford will continue to circulate and metamorphose for many years to come, providing what Nicola Watson aptly calls in her concluding piece, 'a reservoir of creativity' (97).

Katherine Scheil is Professor of English at the University of Minnesota. She is the author of *The Taste of the Town: Shakespearian Comedy and the Early Eighteenth-Century Theatre* (2003), *She Hath Been Reading: Women and Shakespeare Clubs in America* (2012), and *Imagining Shakespeare's Wife: The Afterlife of Anne Hathaway* (2018).

Notes

1. Nick Asbury, *Exit Pursued by a Badger: An Actor's Journey Through History with Shakespeare* (London: Oberon Books, 2009), 26–27.
2. Readers might appreciate the irony in the fact that the chapters in this volume originated at a Shakespeare Association of America seminar on the topic of 'Stratford', held in Seattle, Washington in 2010 – perhaps the most geographically distant locale in the U.S. from Stratford.
3. The Shakespeare   Birthplace Trust, for instance, offers a guidebook of all five properties in French, Spanish, Italian, German, Russian, Japanese and Mandarin. The Birthplace Trust properties encourage group visits, even offering after hours options for 'intimate access' to the Shakespeare Houses, with options for champagne receptions, candle-lit tours, costumed guides and performances of excerpts from Shakespeare by actors. Shakespeare Birthplace Trust Group Visits and Tours mailer, 2012–13.
4. Theodore Bacon, *Delia Bacon: A Biographical Sketch* (Cambridge, Mass: Riverside Press, 1888), 235.
5. Bacon, 241. Letter to Sophia Hawthorne, August 1856.

Chapter 1

Helen Faucit and the Shakespeare Memorial Theatre, Stratford-upon-Avon, 1879

Christy Desmet

On 23 April 1879, the first performance at the original Shakespeare Memorial Theatre in Stratford-upon-Avon took place. The play was *Much Ado About Nothing*, the Beatrice sixty-five-year-old Helen Faucit, long semi-retired from the stage and living life fully as Mrs Theodore Martin. During her long reign on the stage, Faucit had come to stand for the essence of womanliness, both in her Shakespearean impersonations and in her own life; she was, by this point, also considered a figure of national significance. This chapter considers the role played by Faucit in the 1879 festivities, looking at the performance of *Much Ado* through several textual lenses to explore what Helen Faucit meant to Stratford and what the Stratford experience meant to her.

Notes for this section begin on page 20.

Shakespeare, Stratford, England

In histories of Stratford's Memorial Theatre, the inaugural performance of *Much Ado* does not enjoy particular prominence. Ruth Ellis, whose book was published in 1948, moves quickly past the early days in her effort to depict the Theatre's – and Stratford's – fortunes as part of a national history. The significant milestones in town and gown's mutual chronicle are, quite naturally, the fire that destroyed the original theatre structure (1926) and the establishment of Elisabeth Scott's new, more modern and somewhat controversial building (1932), landmarks that epitomise an ongoing rise-and-fall pattern in the enterprise's efforts to do justice to their secular saint and to solidify his hometown's claim to be the keeper of the Bard's eternal flame. But Ellis's account of Stratford's, Shakespeare's and the Theatre's rise to national prominence is framed and sustained by a complementary account of the role played by England's experience of the two world wars in the Memorial Theatre's history and, concomitantly, the role played by Stratford in sustaining the English people during times of national crisis. Of course, war had an immediate effect on the theatre to the extent that it created a shortage of actors and actresses, as well as of paying customers. But more pertinently, during the Second World War, particularly, according to Ellis, town and theatre assumed an active role in supporting the English people. Stratford, although largely protected from the bombings, took in waves of refugees from nearby Coventry and Birmingham. On a more spiritual level, the festival served England's soldiers through Shakespeare's 'power to fortify and exalt the human heart':

> Most of the young men then bearing the brunt of the war passed through Stratford on their way to and from the battlefields, the fighting ships and planes. Few of them could have given anything like a coherent account of Shakespeare's answer to their needs, but some of them have stated categorically that they could not have come sanely through the invasion of Europe without that contact with Shakespeare's mind.[1]

The book concludes with a paean to the essentially English quality of Stratford and its ability to preserve and transmit to all English citizens the wholesome ethos of its native Bard and the rustic community he chose to call home.[2]

Such an understanding of Shakespeare's historical function brings together an idyllic view of England, and particularly

Warwickshire, as expressed by critics such as Arthur Quiller-Couch and analysed by Terence Hawkes, with the more overtly nationalistic view of Shakespeare offered by contemporaneous works such as E.M.W. Tillyard's *Shakespeare's History Plays* (1946).[3] A closer look at the inaugural festivities surrounding the Theatre's opening in 1879, however, will show how a more focused view of the event and its participants ratifies, but only partly, this post-war master narrative.

Much Ado About Nothing, 23 April 1879: The Performance in Context

To an extent, the tone of the original Memorial Shakespeare Theatre's inaugural festivities is consistent with the gala opening of the new Memorial Theatre in 1932. The 1932 celebration was marked by solemn ceremony, the breaking of the flags at the Theatre (rather than at Bridge Street, as was usual), with Sir Frank Benson, former director of the Shakespeare Festival, giving the toast of the 'Immortal Memory' at New Place (Ellis 1948, 67). That occasion was also marked by the appearance of the Prince of Wales by air, who – accompanied by the Mayor, Sir Archibald Flower, in mayoral robes and chains – opened and dedicated the Theatre. But the substance of the Prince's speech will suggest at least one important divergence between the earlier and later ceremonial events. The Prince says:

> Shakespeare was above all things an Englishman. He loved his country with a great and passionate love, and his magic verse not only breathes the air of the country, the air of our long still summer afternoons, but strikes back into the very heart of our history with all its pageantry and daring. We feel proud that the distinctive atmosphere of old England is kept alive here so that our visitors may capture our essence and take away with them living memories. (quoted in Ellis 1948, 68)

Minus the royal presence of the Prince of Wales, the 1879 celebration had emphasised Englishness in a slightly different way, by celebrating Shakespeare not only through his native home, but also through the body and reputation of actress Helen Faucit.

Stratford was, to a large extent, the hero of the 1879 festivities. The town's suitability as the national home for a theatre devoted to Shakespeare was hotly debated in the press. As the *Daily Telegraph* complained after the Shakespeare Birthday play, Stratford, its Theatre, and its celebrations were very much a local affair. The Memorial Theatre's Board of Governors, especially at this early stage, was com-

prised almost entirely of Stratford dignitaries, and Stratford's investment in and control of the Theatre's development raised the hackles
of Londoners who felt that the only appropriate place for a theatre
dedicated to Shakespeare would be the city. As the Memorial Theatre
prepared to open, the *Daily Telegraph* declared that 'They have no
mandate to speak in the name of the public or to invest with the
attribute of a national undertaking a little mutual admiration club'
of local yokels (quoted in Ellis 1948, 10).[4] Despite these criticisms
from London, however, the Memorial Theatre and the annual Birthday play were both celebrated within a Stratford ethos. A complete
and detailed account of the opening night performance and the surrounding festivities can be found in the *Stratford-upon-Avon Herald*,
25 April 1879. The article describes speeches, picnics, fireworks and
other family entertainment – largely outdoors, and persisting in spite
of the doggedly inclement weather. An illustration of the event in *The
Graphic* brings home the importance of Stratford itself by placing its
images of the Theatre within a collage of vignettes depicting the city
and its nascent tourist industry (Illustration 1.1).

This composite image from *The Graphic* shows (at bottom) spectators in the gallery overlooking the stage, watching the initial performance of *Much Ado*. Above are the Edward VI School and New Place
(seen almost from the perspective of the Shakespeare Institute on
Church Street); the Theatre itself, shrouded in mist and viewed from
the opposite bank of the Avon; and two gentlemen contemplating
the Shakespeare monument in Trinity Church. This was an event
more than a performance, or perhaps more precisely, an ongoing
community performance that unfolded in leisurely time across an
expansive, idyllic space. A not unsympathetic review in the *Daily
News*, although waxing ironic about the weather, also depicted Stratford as practically bursting with civic pride, noting in particular 'the
gay aspect of the houses, which not only in the main thoroughfares,
but in the poorest streets in the suburbs along the Avon side, are
hanging out flags and green garlands in honour of the occasion.'
At the inaugural luncheon as well, a company of star-studded aristocrats were greeted with pomp and circumstance by the association president C.E. Flower, who at 'half-past two ascended the stairs,
preceded by two macebearers in official gowns, bearing upon their
shoulders the brazen and glittering tokens of municipal authority.'[5]

Describing the inaugural performance of *Much Ado*, the
Stratford-upon-Avon Herald focuses first on the theatre building as a

Illustration 1.1. 'The Shakespeare Memorial Festival at Stratford-upon-Avon', *The Graphic*, 25 April 1879; by permission of the Folger Shakespeare Library.

ceremonial place. Constructed in a medieval-Victorian style of rather bright red brick (which, defenders said, would mellow over time), the structure sported turrets and towers; inside, it was filled with gold braid and red velvet and seated 800 people. On this night the mood was excited, the audience – which the *Daily Telegraph* intimated, probably wrongly, was composed primarily of Stratford citizens – apparently felt that they were part of a momentous event. The theatrical space itself was well decorated; 'a choice selection of exotic plants and shrubs, tastefully arranged ... imparted to the house quite a refreshing appearance.' The orchestra was constituted from 'a picked body of performers from the principal London theatres, under the direction of Mr. Barnard', who was also the composer of the 'Shakespearian Overture'.[6] Next came the unveiling of the Theatre's tour-de-force drop curtain, which was designed by William Roxby Beverley:[7]

> Another loud and long-continued outburst of applause greeted the rising of the curtain, which exhibited to the view the fine drop-scene by Mr. Beverley. This is indeed a work of art, the design being unique and the scene most artistically treated. The scene represents Queen Elizabeth in her carriage, going to the Globe Theatre, to witness a new play of Shakespeare's. In the foreground is Alleyn, a great friend of the bard's, who is talking to the Earl of Leicester, and standing near him is the Earl of Southampton. They are supposed to be having a chat respecting the play, before leaving their horses with their pages and entering the theatre. The scene is admirably conceived, and most successfully depicted, the various personages being very efficiently portrayed.[8]

The charming antiquarianism of this apocryphal scene aside, the drop curtain makes an interesting meta-comment on the ongoing salvos between Stratford and London regarding the proper home for a national Shakespearean theatre – a debate that Charles Edward Flower, the Stratford mayor and principal force behind the Theatre's establishment, did nothing to smooth over in his public remarks on the occasion by celebrating the 'respectable nobodies' who succeeded where the 'somebodies' from elsewhere could not, in establishing an appropriate memorial theatre to Shakespeare.[9] (In his Sunday sermon at Trinity Church, the Reverend Stopford Brooke, himself a Shakespeare editor and critic, added his own acerbic comments to the mix.)[10]

In the scene depicted on the drop curtain, Elizabeth is going to the Globe, which by metonymy becomes linked to the Stratford Memorial Theatre so that the Memorial Theatre becomes, in effect, the natural heir to Shakespeare's 'original' theatre. Interesting as well is the depiction of this royal theatrical progress as a neighborhood meet-and-greet, as off to the side Edward Alleyn, improbably enough, chats familiarly with the Earls of Leicester and Southampton. In a similar, although perhaps more ironic vein, the *Illustrated Sporting and Dramatic News* review of *Much Ado* is prefaced with a cartoon of Will Shakespeare and Barry Sullivan, the festival director, huddling under an umbrella and exchanging Shakespearean quips about the inclement weather (Illustration 1.2).[11]

Illustration 1.2. Illustrated Sporting and Dramatic News, 3 May 1979; by permission of Christy Desmet

The following events also projected a charmingly local ethos. American entertainer Kate Field, who lived in Stratford and had 'long worked for the cause', gave the dedicatory address (Kemp and Trewin 1953, 8),[12] which was written by the venerable London dramatist John Westland Marston.[13] She was led onto the stage by Mr F.B. Chatterton of the Theatre Royal, Drury Lane, who was also one of the original governors of the Memorial Theatre and the director of this festival.

Finally, the curtain rose to renewed applause, and *Much Ado About Nothing* commenced. The cast contained a mix of venerable and rising actors with London ties. Barry Sullivan, the festival director who also played the part of Benedick, was a Shakespearean actor known for his natural acting style. In 1855, he had performed with

Faucit at the Haymarket Theatre in *The Lady of Lyons* and *As You Like It*, in which he played Jacques (*DNB*). Although a correspondent for *The New York Times* credited Sullivan with merely 'a wide provincial reputation', this characterisation sells Faucit's leading man short.[14] Luigi Lablache, grandson of the famous opera singer and grandfather of actor Stewart Granger, played Don Pedro. Claudio was Edward Compton, son of Henry Compton, and Leonato was played by Shakespearean actor John Ryder.[15] Ellen Wallis (1856–1940) was a young actress active at Drury Lane Theatre in the 1870s; she played Hero, then took over from Faucit the role of Beatrice in Stratford after the opening night. For a local touch, Stratford citizens played various attendants and the members of Dogberry's watch. Sullivan's personal commitment to the Theatre and Festival – he worked without compensation, made a handsome donation and may have paid for the lodging of his actors – also gave to the whole event a warm, neighbourly feeling. This was the company that Helen Faucit joined on 23 April 1879 for the Shakespeare Birthday performance of *Much Ado About Nothing*, appearing for 'one night only' in the part of Beatrice.

Helen Faucit as Stratford's Beatrice

By the time she played Beatrice to Barry Sullivan's Benedick, Faucit was sixty-five years old. She had been semi-retired from the stage since her marriage in 1851 and more emphatically retired for nine years; she had last played Beatrice for 'farewell' performances in Glasgow and Edinburgh in November 1869 and at Manchester, with an inferior Benedick, in November 1871. But her appearance at Stratford was regarded as an historic event, a tribute to the greatest actress of her generation, who had brought to life the women of the great Bard. Helen Faucit was invited to perform in Stratford as a venerable public figure, to give the occasion and enterprise national legitimacy. The provincialism of Stratford was overstated on both sides of the debate about a national Shakespeare theatre. As noted above, the opening cast was certainly reputable; Beverley, the creator of the Theatre's drop curtain, Barnard, the conductor and many members of the orchestra were associated with London theatre; Marston and Chatterton were major London theatrical luminaries; and a fair number of aristocrats attended the opening luncheon.[16] It is true, nevertheless, that Faucit was identified by the media specifically as a *national* dramatic heroine of venerable vintage. The

Illustrated Sporting and Dramatic News reported that 'the comedy *Much Ado About Nothing* [was] ... selected to enable us to see Helen Faucit once more on the stage in a part she made greatly her own.' *The New York Times* referred to Faucit grandly as 'a historic person-age connected with the stage'; the local *Stratford-upon-Avon-Herald* noted that 'it was a source of considerable gratification to all that on this occasion Mrs. Theodore Martin (Helen Faucit) should have kindly consented to appear in the character of Beatrice. Her appear-ance created quite a *furore*: the applause was again and again taken up, the audience exhibiting the utmost enthusiasm.'[17]

By all accounts, the inaugural performance of *Much Ado* was a success. If treated ambivalently by some critics – a 'particularly hostile' critic for the *Era* complained that she was artificial and old-fashioned in her pictorial style of acting[18] – Faucit's performance was nevertheless well-received by her larger audience. The *Stratford-upon-Avon Herald*, which perhaps might be excused for a touch of hyperbole on account of civic pride, reported that:

> Mrs. Theodore Martin played with consummate skill; in fact she delighted the audience with her matchless impersonation of the haughty, sarcastic Beatrice. Her performances were as clever as they were unique, and a rich treat was experienced by all who were for-tunate enough to be present. During the progress of the play Mrs. Martin was frequently and heartily applauded, and at the close of the second act nothing but her appearance before the curtain would sat-isfy the audience; she then received a perfect ovation. At the conclu-sion of the performance a shower of bouquets testified to the great pleasure her acting had afforded.

The *Illustrated Sporting and Dramatic News*, however, concurs: 'Mrs. Martin (Miss Helen Faucit), Miss Wallis, and Mr. Barry Sullivan were received with enthusiastic applause, and the lady first-named received an ovation of the most gratifying description. Her perfor-mance, I need hardly say, was one of the highest order of histrionic merit, and her reappearance, after so long an absence on the boards, excited the greatest interest.' Helen Faucit was great, but she was also offered up as a museum piece, a living legend.

While in the context of the 1879 festivities, Faucit clearly func-tioned as a national monument, what the performance meant to Helen herself is another question altogether. Helen Faucit had been involved with a 'fund-raising benefit for a national Shakespeare monument' at Drury Lane Theatre in June 1863 (Carlisle 2000, 209). She also had agreed to act in the Shakespeare Tercentenary of 1864 – her husband was active in both the London and Stratford committees – but then withdrew when French actress Stella Colas was selected to play Juliet, leaving Faucit with the role of Rosalind (see Carlisle 2000, 209–10).[19] Planning for the 1879 Festival began shortly after the Tercentennial's conclusion,[20] with Sir Theodore Martin again being involved,[21] and for that event, Helen's attitude had changed. She took an active and businesslike interest in the Festival's development and threw herself enthusiastically into the Bardolatry of the moment and into her own historic contributions to the Shakespeare myth. Analysing Faucit's role in the inaugural festivities for the Shakespeare Memorial Theatre and the significance of that event for both actress and audience involves triangulating several sources. Aside from theatre reviews, the actress's career is refracted through at least three additional sources. First, there are the samples of Faucit's abundant correspondence that are housed in rare book libraries. Second, there are Faucit's theatrical reminiscences in her essays of Shakespearean criticism, published separately in *Blackwood's Magazine* and then as a volume in 1885, as *On Some of Shakespeare's Female Characters*. Besides her memory, Faucit relies on letters and her journal. Finally there is the 1900 biography, *Helena Faucit (Lady Martin)*, published after Helen's death by her husband Sir Theodore Martin. The relationship of the last two texts, in particular, is complex. Martin quotes from Helen's correspondence, much of which does not survive; from her journal, which also does not survive; from Helen's published essays on Shakespeare's female characters; and from theatre reviews collected by Helen and by Martin himself. The rich intertextual relations among these texts complicate further any attempt to figure the place of Helen Faucit in the history of the Shakespeare Memorial Theatre and Festival.

As she prepared for the performance of *Much Ado*, Faucit corresponded at some length with Charles Edward Flower, the brewer-mayor of Stratford who was the moving force behind the building of the Theatre, picture gallery, and library and who devoted much income and energy to realising that dream. On 28 March, she writes to advise Flower on his promotion of the gala event and on filling the house for the opening performance, when prices were higher than usual:

Dear Mr. Flower,

    I think you should mark more distinctly in your file that the Beatrice on the opening night will not be the Beatrice in the second representation of the play – otherwise people may put off their visit to Stratford, preferring the 'regular prices' & thinking to have the same for their money.[22]

On 20 April 1879, she writes to Flower with the news that she is suffering from a toothache and giving information about her imminent arrival at Stratford and the arrival of her costume directly from London.[23] As one might expect, Faucit is quite businesslike, as befits a professional actress. For although there is some implicit disagreement between her and Sir Theodore on this point, Faucit never regarded herself as having quit the stage. At the same time, however, Faucit seems to enter fully into the social, neighbourly spirit of the Festival, much as she did in her local neighbourhoods in Onslowe Square and in Wales. As Peter Holland has argued, theatres can function as sites for social memory, the kind that involves shared experience with persons who already have a connection with one another.[24] In many important ways – not the least of which was the ongoing involvement of the Flower family – the establishment of the Shakespeare Memorial Theatre was a product of just such a social memory, and the most extensive letter written by Faucit to C.E. Flower shows that her sense of that community persisted, even long after the 1879 Festival. In 1891, twelve years later, Faucit writes:

Dear Mr. Flower,

I have too long left unacknowledged your very kind letter, for which indeed I thank you.

I have been a little overweighted with correspondence since the year began & not being very well, have been obliged to let some drop in abeyance. I am pleased that you and Mrs. Flower like my letter on 'Hermione.' As with the other Shakespearean characters, I have felt obliged to make a kind of resumé of the whole play, and 'The Winter's Tale' I found very difficult to cope with ... I had no idea that my old friend Mrs. Flower Adams was your cousin. I used to meet her at a mutual friend's house, Mrs. Braysher, another keen lover of the drama & admirer of the then youthful representations of the heroines of the stage. I remember, as it were only yesterday dear Mrs. Adams asking me if I had made a study of Greek sculpture. I replied, no – that I had only seen it in books & engravings. She said she thought I had, because I posed on the forward foot as the statue, as the Greeks always did. I explained that this on my part was accident, as I know no better – she would have it 'not so, – but instinct.' I never forgot her criticism & have always followed it up. She was so cultured and possessed such fine feeling, that to please her was a great delight to me ...[25]

Offering Flower a copy of her *Blackwood*'s essay on Hermione for the Shakespeare Memorial Library, which had opened in 1880, Faucit not only makes a generous offer of a complimentary book, but she also makes the contact with her correspondent both warm and personal. As is typical of Faucit in her criticism as well as in her correspondence, she brings together imaginatively the past and present through memories of friends that place herself and Flower within a social network. Faucit remembers Mrs. Braysher, the friend who not only supervised Faucit's bouquets early on in her career, but also acted as her companion during her illness of 1844 and became a regular at the Martins' Shakespearean soirees in the 1860s. Faucit also establishes a personal connection with Flower by remarking on his kinship with another of her old friends, Sarah Flower Adams – actress, author, poet, supporter of human rights for women and working-class people, and author of the hymn, 'Nearer, My God, to Thee.'[26] Helen Faucit apparently kept in her heart a warm thought for Stratford, its Shakespeare Theatre and the Festival's local patron; and she incorporated Charles Flower into her inner circle with the same enthusiasm and grace as she did when hosting Shakespearean readings at the Martins' Onslowe Square home, which were attended by such luminaries as rising actor Henry Irving.[27]

The Stratford Festival and its inaugural performance of *Much Ado* are also addressed by Faucit, with the benefit of nostalgic hindsight, in the penultimate essay of *On Some of Shakespeare's Female Characters*. Faucit's remarks on Beatrice are written between 1882 and 1885 for John Ruskin, the author of *Sesame and Lilies*, which celebrates the ennobling influence on man that women exert: 'infallibly faithful and wise counselors, – incorruptibly just and pure examples – strong always to sanctify, even when they cannot save.'[28] Interestingly, the essay's analysis of Beatrice's 'sanctifying' effect on Benedick edges toward a proto-feminist stance that is somewhat at odds not only with Ruskin's concept of redemptive femininity, but also with Faucit's own legendary status as the embodiment of Shakespearean womanhood.[29] For her Beatrice, in the essay at least, is almost 'manly' in her response to the slander against Hero, and her 'sanctified' effect on Benedick seems to result in the theatrically disputed command, 'Kill Claudio': 'When Claudio, assuming conscious guilt from [Hero's] silence, went on with his charge, I could hardly keep still. My feet tingled, my eyes flashed lightning upon the princes and Claudio. Oh that I had been her brother, her cousin, and not a powerless woman!' (Faucit 1899, 318).

Faucit's self-presentation is further framed, however, by her account of two other performances in *Much Ado About Nothing*. The first was her debut in the role, which was also Charles Kemble's farewell to the stage. In this performance, according to Faucit's self-representation, she was a timid ingénue swept up in a role she was hardly qualified to perform, but sustained by her paternal mentor, Kemble, and caught up tearfully in the emotion of his departure. When asked by the great Kemble what he could offer her as a remembrance, Helen asked, through her sobs, for 'the book from which you studied Benedick' (Faucit 1899, 234). Charles Kemble gave Helen Shakespeare editions that had belonged to his daughter Fanny Kemble, Faucit's immediate great predecessor on the English Shakespearean stage. (She and Sir Theodore preserved them, and they reside today in the Shakespeare Centre Library in Stratford.) Faucit's description of her final performance in the role of Beatrice at Stratford in 1879 is less personal, less emotional – almost more like a theatrical review. Her account is generally in harmony with the reviews, stressing the emotional fervour and local pride that fuelled the Festival. She recalls:

> I had watched with interest the completion of this most appropriate tribute to the memory of our supreme poet. The local enthusiasm, which would not rest until it had placed upon the banks of his native stream a building in which his best plays might be from time to time presented, commanded my warm sympathy. It is a beautiful building; and when, standing beside it, I looked upon the church wherein all that was mortal of the poet is laid, and on the other hand, my eyes rested on New Place, where he died, a feeling more earnest, more reverential, came over me than I have experienced even in Westminster Abbey, in Santa Croce, or in any other resting place of the mighty dead. (Faucit 1899, 327)

Tellingly, Faucit's tour of the Memorial Theatre replicates the newspapers' sense that the Birthday play performance was part of a city tour, as her eye moves from the vantage point of the Memorial Theatre to rest on the Avon, Trinity Church and New Place. In her mind, these 'sacred sights' substitute for (and supplant) the known pilgrimage sites of Westminster Abbey (which in her private role as Mrs Martin, she knew well) and the Basilica of Santa Croce. Bardolatry is combined with a certain Chamber of Commerce pride in the city of Stratford-upon-Avon.

Faucit's further remarks also parallel the newspaper accounts, recognising the historic nature of her own appearance on the stage while also capturing the excitement generated by the event:

> It was a deep delight to me to be the first to interpret on that spot one of my master's brightest creations. Everything conspired to make the occasion happy. From every side of Shakespeare's county, from London, from remote provinces, came people to witness that performance. The characters were well supported, and the fact that we were acting in Shakespeare's birthplace, and to inaugurate his memorial theatre, seemed to inspire us all. Every turn of playful humour, every flash of wit, every burst of strong feeling told; and it is a great pleasure to me to think, that on that spot and on that occasion I made my last essay to present a living portraiture of the Lady Beatrice. (Faucit 1899, 327)

Here, Faucit skilfully connects the import of the performance for Shakespeare and his birthplace to its significance in her own theatrical history. The remainder of Helen's letter/essay, somewhat surprisingly, veers off into a technical discussion of stage business. Faucit begins by complimenting the Memorial Theatre's 'judicious' use of 'accessories', which basically means scenery: 'The stage, being of moderate size, admitted of no elaborate display. But the scenes were appropriate and well painted, the dresses were well chosen, and the general effect was harmonious – satisfying the eye, without distracting the spectators' mind from the dialogue and the play of character' (Faucit 1899, 327). While newspaper reports focused on the decorative aspects of Stratford's Memorial Theatre, Faucit herself seems to be championing a more emotional and less scenic theatre, which is confirmed by a final reminiscence of her performance opposite Macready in Milton's almost anti-theatrical *Comus*. Faucit seems to be caught not only between old and newer standards of verisimilitude, but also to be focusing, if surreptitiously, on the actor's craft rather than on the Festival's lavish rituals. Faucit 'gets' the Stratford Festival, but she merges her understanding of its significance for Stratford with a sense of the *Much Ado* performance's significance for her own legend. This is an extremely self-conscious critical performance.

About the Stratford performance of 1879, Theodore Martin has relatively little to say. He is content to quote from Faucit's Letter on Beatrice, focusing primarily on her sense of the crowd (a melting pot of locals, Londoners and visitors from 'remote provinces') and her rapport with the audience caused by their mutual excitement over 'the fact that we were acting in Shakespeare's birthplace' (Martin

1900, 357) surrounding this nugget of text are mundane accounts of the trip, the persistent rain, and the difficulties of engaging a carriage in bad weather, which led Lord Stoneleigh to donate his own vehicle to the cause of carrying Helen Faucit home safely. The whole event is subordinated as well to Martin's running account of Helen's personal life, but more pointedly, to Martin's description of Faucit's readings, some for charity and some for social purposes. Like many Shakespearean actors before her – Charles Kemble, Sarah Siddons, Fanny Kemble – after the end of her active professional career, Faucit gave readings of Shakespeare, an activity that is poised decorously between acting on stage and private reading, an activity suitable for ladies and gentlemen of good social standing. In this context, the *Much Ado* performance becomes less important and less professional than it seems in the reviews, Faucit's correspondence or her published Shakespearean criticism.

Coda

Throughout her long and illustrious acting career, Helen Faucit had become identified with Shakespeare's female characters and they with her. Her embodiment for audiences of an essentially English femininity and her display of that essence on the stage undoubtedly figured into the serendipitous selection of Faucit to play a Shakespearean comic heroine who had been born under a dancing star in the town that was attempting to establish itself as an English version of Shakespeare's Messina – quiet, insular, but perfect in its own way through its proprietary association with Shakespeare. On a more poignant note, the connection between Helen Faucit and Shakespeare could be taken only so far in Stratford. After Faucit's death, Sir Theodore donated Helen's promptbooks to the Shakespeare Memorial Library and the well-known portrait of her by Rudolph Lehmann to the Picture Gallery. To Trinity Church he gave a green marble pulpit decorated with sculptured figures of saints – Saint Helena was said to resemble Helen Faucit. But when Martin wished to have a copy of the memorial of Faucit that was in Llantysilio Church (near the Martins' Welsh home) placed opposite the Shakespeare bust in Trinity Church, Marie Corelli, the novelist, Juliet from the 1864 Tercentennial and local Stratford celebrity, kicked up such a fuss that Martin eventually acceded.

Illustration 1.3. John Henry Foley, Relief of Helen Faucit; by permission of the Courtauld Institute of Art, London.

It was, as Faucit's biographer Carol Jones Carlisle notes, Sir Theodore Martin's biography that would become Helen Faucit's final loving 'monument' (Illustration 1.3; see Carlisle 2000, 269–72).

Christy Desmet (1954–2018) was Josiah Meigs Distinguished Teaching Professor at the University of Georgia, author of *Reading Shakespeare's Characters: Rhetoric, Ethics, and Identity* (1992) and editor of several collections of essays on Shakespearean appropriation: *Shakespeare and Appropriation* (with Robert Sawyer, 1999), *Harold Bloom's Shakespeare* (with Robert Sawyer, 2001), *Shakespearean Gothic* (with Anne Williams, 2009) and *Helen Faucit* (2011).

Notes

1. Ruth Ellis, *The Shakespeare Memorial Theatre* (London: Winchester Publications, 1948), 104.

2. Similar sentiments can be found in the two forewords to *Shakespeare Memorial Theatre: A Photographic Record, 1948–1950*, written by Ivor Brown and Anthony Quayle (London: M. Reinhardt, 1950).

3. E.M.W. Tillyard, *Shakespeare's History Plays* (New York: Macmillan, 1946).

4. Other snippets from the reviews can be found in M.C. Day and J.C. Trewin, *The Shakespeare Memorial Theatre* (London and Toronto: J.M. Dent & Sons, 1932), 45–48.

5. *Daily News*, 24 April 1879.

6. In 1880, 'Mr. Bernard' is listed as the conductor of the orchestra for performances of *As You Like It* at the Imperial and Lyceum Theatres and as conductor of the orchestra at Drury Lane Theatre. See, for instance, *Punch*, 6 March 1880, 11.

7. William Roxby Beverley (ca.1814–1889) was a great English scene painter who worked in Manchester and in London at the Princess's, Lyceum and Drury Lane Theatres. He worked for Charles Kean in particular *The Concise Oxford Companion to the Theatre*, second edition. (Oxford and New York: Oxford University Press, 1992).

8. *Stratford-upon-Avon Herald*, 25 April 1879, from Volume 1 of 'Theatre Records', in the Shakespeare Centre Library, Shakespeare Birthplace Trust, Stratford-upon-Avon.

9. T.C. Kemp and J.C. Trewin, *The Stratford Festival: A History of the Shakespeare Memorial Theatre* (Birmingham: Cornish Bros., 1953), 7–8.

10. See Kemp and Trewin 1953, 11; and Day and Trewin 1932, 41–42.

11. Shakespeare says, 'Truly, brother Barry, the rain it raineth every day', and Sullivan replies, 'Marry! An a vengeance too, brother Will!'

12. Mary Katherine Keemle Field (1838–1896) was an American journalist, actress and entertainer; she is best known as the object of Anthony Trollope's platonic romantic interest (*Oxford Dictionary of National Biography* [Oxford: Oxford University Press, 2012], http://www.oxforddnb.com/).

13. John Westland Marston (1819–1890) was the author of *The Patrician's Daughter*, in which Helen Faucit had first performed with William Charles Macready at Drury Lane on 10 December 1842.

14. 'Shakespeare's Birthday', *The New York Times*, 27 April 1879. Sullivan got his start in Edinburgh; like other actors, he toured the provinces and was also popular in Ireland. But Sullivan was also active in London theatre and acted abroad; in the mid-1870s, he not only performed at Drury Lane, but also did an ambitious tour of thirty-three cities, including New York, where he played Hamlet (*Oxford Dictionary of National Biography*).

15. Edward Compton (1854–1918), actor and theatre manager, was a seasoned performer at this point. On 27 September 1879, he would set sail with Asta Neilsen for her American tour (*Oxford Dictionary of National Biography*). John Ryder (1814–1885) played with Macready in 1842 – he was Duke Frederick in *As You Like It*, among other roles – and accompanied Macready on his 1848–1849 American tour; in 1845 at the Princess's Theatre, he played Claudius to Macready's

Hamlet, and in the 1850s, he played with Charles Kean (*Oxford Dictionary of National Biography*).

16. See *Daily News*, 24 April 1879.

17. Review of *Much Ado About Nothing*, Shakespeare Memorial Theatre, *Illustrated Sporting and Dramatic News*, 3 May 1879; 'Shakespeare's Birthday', *New York Times*, 27 April 1879; *Stratford-upon-Avon Herald*, 25 April 1879.

18. Carol Jones Carlisle, *Helen Faucit: Fire and Ice on the Victorian Stage* (London: Society for Theatre Research, 2000), 225.

19. The problems and rivalries besetting the Tercentenary celebration, including the beginning of the rivalry between London and Stratford, are detailed in Richard Foulkes, *The Shakespeare Tercentenary of 1864* (London: Society for Theatre Research, 1984); he notes that the theatrical rivalries were widespread and generally blames the theatrics surrounding Faucit's engagement and subsequent withdrawal on her husband (16).

20. See, for instance, 'The Intended Memorial of Shakespeare at Stratford-upon-Avon', *The Times*, 24 March 1864.

21. For instance, when the foundation stone for the Theatre was laid in 1877, in a 'collation' later at New Place, Theodore Martin was one of the people who gave a speech (Day and Trewin 1932), 40.

22. Helen Faucit to C.E. Flower, Folger Shakespeare Library, Y. c. 3840 (5). Perhaps Flower took Faucit's advice. The playbill for the Memorial Theatre's inaugural season stressed that 'Mrs. Theodore Martin' would appear as Beatrice 'for one night only'; see Carol Chillington Rutter, 'Shakespeare's Popular Face: From the Playbill to the Poster', in *The Cambridge Companion to Shakespeare and Popular Culture*, ed. Robert Shaughnessy (Cambridge: Cambridge University Press, 2007), 253.

23. Helen Faucit to C.E. Flower, Folger Shakespeare Library, Y. c. 3840 (4).

24. Peter Holland, 'On the Gravy Train: Shakespeare, Memory, and Forgetting', in *Shakespeare, Memory, and Performance*, ed. Peter Holland (Cambridge: Cambridge University Press, 2006), 207–34.

25. Helen Faucit to C.E. Flower, 13 January 1891, Folger Shakespeare Library, Y. c. 3340 (11).

26. *Oxford Dictionary of National Biography*; see also Carlisle 2000, 71; for Faucit's acquaintance with Sarah Flower Adams, see the diary entry for 4 January 1839, quoted by Sir Theodore Martin, *Helena Faucit (Lady Martin)* (Edinburgh: W. Blackwood and Sons, 1900), 58.

27. Helen and Theodore Martin began hosting 'drawing-room readings' of Shakespeare in 1877, accommodating as many as seventy or eighty guests; Irving first attended in February of 1878 and became a regular guest (see Carlisle 2000, 239).

28. John Ruskin, *Sesame and Lilies*, revised and enlarged edition (1871), xxvi, quoted by Helen Faucit, *On Some of Shakespeare's Female Characters*, sixth edition (Edinburgh and London: William Blackwell and Sons, 1899), 289–90.

29. Here, I am putting into discussion Carol Carlisle's sense that Faucit was at least distanced from, if not wholly disapproving of the 'modern theatre' (Carlisle 2000, 253–55).

Chapter 2
Secret Stratford
Shakespeare's Hometown in Recent Young Adult Fiction

Susanne Greenhalgh

In a number of novels for young people, Shakespeare's hometown, Stratford, serves as location for at least part of the action, its landmarks invested with both narrative and thematic significance. In both fiction and biography Shakespeare's life is often represented as one pragmatically or emotionally split between a Stratford constructed in terms of childhood, marriage, retirement, domesticity and the everyday, and the London of court and theatre, a world of work, achievement, exotic dangers and pleasures. In this dynamic, Stratford embodies the values that Barbara Hodgdon finds evoked by its tourism today.

> Stratford's sites offer images of a perfectly ordered and regulated bourgeois existence, a hermetic world of accumulation, private ownership, and enclosure in which the normal, the commonplace, and the close-at-hand become elevated to museum status. Apparent every-

where, the ideas of home and family, central to everyday life, act as controlling paradigms for reconstructing an idea of life lived under Shakespeare's ruling gaze.[1]

However, as Erica Hateley concludes from her study of Shakespeare-based children's books in terms of gender and cultural capital, 'Shakespeare must literally or symbolically reject his domestic Stratford life in order to lead a successful theatrical, London life.'[2] In so doing, as a number of critics have explored, he often becomes the centre of an alternative theatrical and urban family which, by virtue of its all-male composition, excludes or appropriates feminine presence and agency in ways analogous to the patriarchal 'ruling gaze' that Hodgdon finds embodied in the heritage sites of Stratford. According to Hateley there is indeed only one story in youth fiction featuring Shakespeare the man, the 'boy-meets-Shakespeare' plot, which in turn encodes a crucial, gendered distinction between the experience of male and female characters and thus the focalisation available to young male or female readers:

> Feminine characters are excluded from symbolic relationships with the playwright often, paradoxically, by virtue of being Shakespeare's actual daughter ... not only is feminine subjectivity depicted as ideally separate from Shakespeare, but 'Shakespeare' is also made a resolutely patriarchal discourse, which is, in part, made possible because of its difference and distance from femininity.[3]

Kate Chedgzoy observes that typically in such novels 'the Shakespearean theatre [is] the scene for boys' journeys towards adulthood.'[4] This theme appears in one of the earliest examples, the popular late-nineteenth-century novel, *Master Skylark*, by the American writer John Bennett.[5] After the Lord Admiral's Men are banned from playing at Stratford a schoolboy follows them to Coventry, where he is kidnapped, apprenticed into a boys' company in London, and befriended by Shakespeare. After many adventures he returns to Stratford, where Shakespeare is holding a party for all his theatre friends to celebrate the purchase of New Place. Although the boy's father initially bars him from his home, Shakespeare stage manages reconciliation and the family is reunited. In the seminal *Cue for Treason*[6] and Gary Blackwood's Shakespeare trilogy, young characters also journey by choice or force of circumstance from their homes and find a surrogate family in the theatre and a substitute parent and mentor in Shakespeare, before finally returning home or building a new life in London.

The myth of Stratford as Shakespeare's loved or rejected home thus makes it a suitable location in writing for the young, where the idea of lost, re-found or substitute homes is so often a central theme or plot device. Lucy Waddey has suggested that, 'Although so deep and subtle a subject as home eludes all final categories, the artistic use of home as both a setting and theme in children's fiction falls into three basic patterns: home as a frame, home as a focus, and home as an evolving reflection of the protagonist.'[7] The meaning of home also changes and develops as young people mature. According to Virginia L. Wolf narratives of home in writing for the young of different ages typically move 'from celebration, to adventure, to memory, to guilt, to irony – from being at home, to attempting to save a home, to internalizing its meaning and value, to recognizing the difficulty of reflecting its meaning and value in one's acts, to having its meaning and value denied.'[8] The complex interplay in youth fiction between Shakespeare as an absentee from his home and family, and his construction as a paternalistic protector of the permanently or temporarily homeless young ensures that Stratford becomes an ambiguous and sometimes contradictory repository of the values conventionally associated with the domestic realm and with the Shakespeare/Stratford myth.

These novels also appear influenced to a degree by contemporary scholarship, such as new data about visits from theatre companies in the years before Shakespeare left for London, which have established the town's position in relation to a number of touring routes.[9] Consequently, as in *Master Skylark,* Stratford is presented as a site of theatrical performance, thereby diminishing the divide between the theatre profession in London and Shakespeare's domestic and financial concerns back home. More significantly for my purposes, all the novels respond with varying degrees of seriousness to the revival of academic interest in Shakespeare and religion, especially his relationship with Catholicism, which emerged controversially in the late 1990s.[10] While religion has featured in previous children's novels about Shakespeare's theatre, notably those of Antonia Forest,[11] the politicisation of religion seems to be a particularly popular element at the beginning of the twenty-first century.[12] Writing about fiction featuring Shakespeare and Queen Elizabeth, Helen Hackett has suggested that 'religion may be taking the place of class as a charged and emotive issue in versions of their double myth.'[13] The same can be said of the versions of the Stratford myth represented by the youth fiction surveyed here. Thus, while Stratford can represent home, family and security, these values are often infiltrated or threatened by a darker secret life that revolves around religious worship and its suppression, so that Shakespeare's hometown is portrayed as dangerous and sometimes deadly. Although on the surface this quiet country backwater appears to be a secure refuge from the dangers brought down from London, whether in the form of plague or conspiracy, it is also revealed as a place harbouring its own deadly hazards and homegrown plots, many of them rooted in religion. According to Naomi Wood, 'Religion in children's literature functions as a mechanism of social ordering, of setting up hermeneutic categories with which to view the world.'[14] In these novels, by contrast, religion is most often viewed as a force that complicates the young person's view of the world and may threaten the security of the home.

In his study of Shakespeare in modern popular culture, Douglas Lanier identifies six 'interlocking mythic narratives' encoded both by Stratford's tourist geography and the fictions of Shakespeare's home life which these settings have inspired: 'Shakespeare the child of Stratford (Birthplace); Shakespeare the learned man (Grammar School); Shakespeare the bourgeois success story (New Place and Nash's House); Shakespeare the patriarch (Hall's Croft); Shakespeare the lover (Anne Hathaway's cottage); Shakespeare the rural villager (Mary Arden's House)'.[15] Collectively, he argues, these narratives construct early modern Stratford as safely pastoral, 'a pre-technological utopian age characterized by the natural rhythms, modest domesticity and time-worn rituals of village life, a distinctively British vision of organic communalism.'[16] However, a more complex picture of Stratford life emerges in the young adult novels discussed here. Stratford is portrayed as a busy town, rather than as a timeless rural enclave, inevitably shaped by the shifting politics of the day. While Shakespeare's house, New Place, is generally portrayed as a place of safety, presided over by a stalwart Anne Hathaway, beyond its walls bigots, spies and assassins prowl, and in some of the stories it is Shakespeare's own political or religious involvement which brings deadly peril to his door. To the six landmarks listed by Lanier as key to the Stratford myth a seventh is added: Holy Trinity Church and its graveyard. Shakespeare's Stratford often becomes a death-haunted place, especially resonant with memories of his young son, Hamnet. While some of the novels discussed here do appear to emphasise 'modest domesticity' and reinstate the pattern of feminine marginalisation that Hateley and Chedgzoy identify, others complicate it by employing a female narrator, or using multiple, differently gendered, narrative voices.

Although linked by their attention to Stratford, all the novels of course have their own distinct generic qualities and intended audience, which inflect their use of the Stratford setting. Terry Deary's *The Lord of the Dreaming Globe* is part of a series originally called 'Tudor Terror' now more neutrally labelled 'Tudor Chronicles'; a spinoff from his multi-million 'Horrible Histories' empire, and aimed at the same 'tween' age range.[17] These use multiple narrators to tell the stories of the Marsdens, a family of mine-owning and story-loving gentry in Durham, and their dangerous adventures in the ever-changing politics of the period. *The Lord of the Dreaming Globe* is set around 1602, as England awaits the regime change that will follow Elizabeth's death, and brings young Will Marsden and his canny serving-girl friend, Meg, to Stratford, to work on Shakespeare's accounts. En route they encounter plotters planning to assassinate Shakespeare, who is revealed as one of Robert Cecil's spies, and an active propagandist for the peaceful accession of James of Scotland to the English throne and the greater religious tolerance this may bring. The climax of the novel reveals that Christopher Marlowe was not killed in Deptford but continued to work under another name as a spy for Elizabeth, writing no more plays, and harbouring murderous intentions towards Shakespeare inspired as much by artistic envy as by the political situation. Throughout, the novel's action is related from the shifting perspectives of Will, Meg, an actor friend and Shakespeare himself.

The novels that might seem closest to preserving the reassuring 'Shakespeare Country' rural motifs identified by Lanier are Carolyn Meyer's *Loving Will Shakespeare*,[18] Jan Mark's *Stratford Boys*,[19] and Michael J. Ortiz's *Swan Town: The Secret Journal of Susanna Shakespeare*,[20] all of which are set almost entirely in Stratford and its immediate surroundings. Both Meyer's and Mark's novels portray a youthful Shakespeare before his permanent departure from his hometown. The former, written in the first person, tells Agnes Hathaway's[21] story from her attendance at Shakespeare's christening in 1564 up to the point of her marriage, and stresses the local work and rituals which shape the passing seasons for a heroine who never goes further afield than Kenilworth and Worcester. *Stratford Boys*, as emphasised by the title, takes place entirely in the town, in 1580, and is a rare example of a contemporary novel depicting Shakespeare as a youth, just out of school and working for the family glove business. The novel's chief concern is with his initiation as a playwright as he rewrites a medieval mystery play to provide a Whitsun entertainment for the townsfolk. *Swan Town*, set in 1597, also centres on playwriting, this time the dreams of Shakespeare's daughter to have her play staged in London. In Susanna's journal Stratford becomes 'Swan Town', a name designed to invoke both the calm, if boring, beauty of its riverside landscape, and her soaring aspirations as a would-be playwright and ardent Catholic, as well as of course referencing the epithet attached to Shakespeare by Ben Jonson in his elegy in the First Folio. By the end of the novel the name also encompasses the legend that swans sing at their death, an image applied to Shakespeare's brother Edmund, who is depicted suffering Catholic martyrdom. The last novel discussed is Celia Rees's *The Fool's Girl* set in 1601.[22] Shakespeare becomes involved with characters from the story which will form the source for *Twelfth Night*, but the play's plot is given a catastrophic sequel in which Viola and her Duke have been killed in a coup by Sebastian and his pirate accomplices, and their daughter Violetta, with Feste, must try to prevent a vengeful Malvolio (now a Jesuit) and recusant Sir Andrew from using a precious Illyrian relic to rouse English Catholics to overthrow Elizabeth. Although much of the action takes place in London, Warwickshire provides the setting for a bloody climax during a performance of *A Midsummer Night's Dream*.

In *Stratford Boys* the town is depicted both as a homely and familiar place, where everyone knows and tolerates each other, and as a community responding nervously to religious, economic and social change. The novel's opening words tellingly construct Shakespeare's home as a changeable, even unstable location: 'The Shakespeares had the builders in again'.[23] Sixteen-year old Shakespeare and his best friend Adrian would have gone to Oxford to study if their fathers' finances had permitted, and the theatre companies have stopped visiting a town in recession, two factors that precipitate the project to put on a play with a rag-tag company of schoolboys and workmen. Written mainly in dialogue the novel rarely directly paints the detailed picture of Stratford attempted in some of the others. Although its action moves between clearly demarcated locations such as the Shakespeare house in Henley Street, the market place, church, and town pubs, the reader is largely left to picture these herself. However, in one key passage more explicit attention is paid to the Stratford setting. The actors are arguing about the details of the play with the kind of literalism about theatre portrayed in *A Midsummer Night's Dream*. One of the company is provoked into a defence of theatrical illusion:

> You have all seen plays yourselves, put on by the London companies. Think back ... Didn't you stand in the yard of the Swan in Bridge Street, in Stratford town, in the County of Warwick, beside Avon River, in England, under an English sky, in English weather, and yet believed you were in France, or Illyria, or Tartary, in broiling heat or icy waste? Before your eyes Englishmen walked on boards of English oak with the windows and walls of the inn behind them, and yet you heard English speech on English tongues and yet understood that these men spoke a foreign language. Now, because it is your own selves who will be treading the boards you can not trust an audience to do the same for you and you can not trust yourselves to make it happen.[24]

This eloquent evocation of the imaginary, transformative journey beyond the confines of Stratford made possible by theatrical performance points forward to Shakespeare's inevitable departure from his home and his future achievements. Although the domestic and working life of Stratford is evoked with lively precision Mark's novel is primarily concerned with the intellectual curiosity and imagination which drive Will to read every book in the town, constantly revise his play and with its successful performance discover his metier, to transform his life by transforming the everyday life around him into theatre. The bringing on stage of his newly born brother Edmund to represent the turning of the play's tragic narrative into comedy through an unexpected birth appropriately embodies the process of turning real life into fiction which the novel celebrates. Shakespeare's hometown may frame him but finally, like everything he experiences, it is primarily the raw material for his art.

In *Loving Will Shakespeare*, which takes the form of Anne's memoir claiming to tell her own and Shakespeare's story, the significance of the setting is underlined by the prologue's heading, 'Stratford-upon-Avon. Warwickshire, England 1611' over lines from Shakespeare's letter announcing that he is leaving London for good. The final chapter is titled 'Coming Home', and summarises the intervening years of absence since their marriage in 1582, including the purchase of New Place after the death of Hamnet. However, most of the novel depicts Anne's home life at Shottery, two miles outside Stratford. Hewlands (now known as Anne Hathaway's Cottage) is depicted as a working farm, ensuring that while the novel participates in the stress on 'feminine and domestic history' that Katherine Scheil has identified as a dominant motif in the afterlives of Shakespeare's wife, its rural cottage milieu is far from pastorally peaceful.[25] Stratford is where Anne goes for neighbours' parties, to deliver her homebrewed ale or to sell the produce from her hives, thus offering some economic independence and escape from her vicious stepmother, as well as encounters with potential lovers. The significance of Stratford as the setting for potential romantic and sexual fulfilment is signalled when she recalls receiving a 'kiss for each of the fourteen arches of the stone bridge that crossed the Avon' from her first lover, before her occasional meetings with the boy she has known since he was a baby blossom into romance in the woods outside the town.[26] As is unsurprising in a novel aimed at teenage girls, Anne's sexuality is not presented as predatory, but sensibly cautious, imbued with romantic longing and desire for a home of her own – one close to all that she knows. She declines the chance of an elopement to the North Country with an attractive poacher and, constrained by the risk of a summons before Stratford's Bawdy Court, she is still a virgin when she first makes love with the teenage Will. However, the home she ultimately wins for herself brings sadness and frustration as well as sexual fulfilment and motherhood. Although her retrospective account of her life suggests that she continued 'loving Will Shakespeare' long after he became 'but occasional visitor to his own home',[27] it also reveals her reluctance to leave Stratford or even hear about Shakespeare's life in London. For Anne, therefore, Stratford is her chosen frame and focus, as well as the means by which her evolving character is revealed to the reader. As she muses at the end of the book, Shakespeare's absence has given her autonomy, and she and her daughters have had 'our own company, our own lives' in 'the splendid house on Chapel Street',[28] but the novel's structure keeps this feminine home life hidden and unvoiced.

For Susanna Shakespeare in *Swan Town*, which is aimed at a slightly younger readership, her Stratford home is a 'sleepy town that would tether me to a life as narrow as any barn.'[29] In her entries in her secret journal, punctuated by colourful oaths expressive of her frustration with provincial life, she rails against the kind of traditionalism accepted as inevitable in Meyer's novel: 'Here in Stratford, sons follow their fathers year after year. Blacksmiths beget blacksmiths, cobblers beget cobblers, and women and girls bring harvest after harvest to kitchen day after day ... this silly patch of a town.'[30]

While Anne's life conforms to the pattern outlined by Hateley in which the main reader position on offer is acceptance of a prescribed domestic role, Susanna's progress is presented in more deliberately anachronistic terms. She is consistently portrayed as her father's true heir (especially after the death of Hamnet), through her desire to perform and write plays. In *Loving Will Shakespeare*, theatrical activity such as visits from acting companies or attendance at the Earl of Leicester's entertainments for the Queen at Kenilworth are primarily presented as male concerns, stages in the process that will inevitably take Shakespeare away from Stratford. In *Swan Town* they are grasped by Susanna as occasions to further her own eventually successful plans to perform her play on the stage of the Globe by cross-dressing and acting. However, her two London trips, the first to save her uncle Edmund from the consequences of trying to revive a play about the Catholic martyr Thomas More, the second which sees her mother arrested outside the Globe and imprisoned in Newgate as a recusant, are also the occasions for her first meeting, then developing romance, with her future husband, the Puritan physician John Hall. The novel's final scene takes place in London, after Shakespeare has been saved by his brother Edmund dying in his place. Shakespeare's words of parting as his extended family return to Stratford are full of references to nature and growth, demarcating the country town from the aspirations represented by London, 'this town of steeples': 'Now, Anne, you look after my gardens, and watch for the canker in the spring roses ... And you, John Hall ... get those herb gardens going in the spring. An early start is the shortest way to a long harvest.'[31] Susanna's backward look sees him finally 'swallowed up by the crowds and towers of the non-awakened city',[32] while she disappears forever into the 'long harvest' of a hidden, undocumented life in Stratford. While the novel attempts to flesh out the epitaph on the historical Susanna's grave in Holy Trinity Church, that she was 'witty above her sex, but that's not all / Wise to salvation ... / Something of Shakespeare was in that', Susanna's fate, like Anne's, lies back home in 'Swan Town', in an ecumenical marriage as the Catholic wife of a Puritan. As with Anne, her home, not London, is the primary frame, focus and reflection of her development in the novel, but it is a home that is not purely defined as a domestic realm but one tested and strengthened both by her departures from it and by being exposed to the dangers brought about by the religious convictions of its inhabitants.

Gardens and the natural world more generally also appear as part of the Shakespearean/Stratfordian landscape created in *The Lord of the Dreaming Globe* and *The Fool's Girl*. Walled and fruitful Shakespeare's blessed plot becomes not simply pastoral but almost an 'other Eden, demi-paradise', symbolic of a realm supposedly free from division or danger.[33] However, unlike Anne and Susanna, the young protagonists are visitors rather than native to Stratford. Will and Meg first enter New Place through the back gate and meet Shakespeare's wife in a 'warm sunny garden' in which the 'grass was soft and the flowers rich in colour and perfume.'[34] In *The Fool's Girl* the Illyrian refugees are also only temporary guests, and the garden's 'fine plot, with sunny walls for vines and fruit trees'[35] offers a respite from the disaster that has overtaken their own home. As in *Swan Town*, it is presented as Shakespeare's own creation, but one that in reality is not safe from the outside world. Having been recruited by Robert Cecil to undertake espionage, Shakespeare is rewarded with cartloads of rare plants and seedlings, including the first tulip in Stratford. Arriving in such profusion they threaten to overwhelm the existing ecology and alert his enemies. Shakespeare takes Violetta and Feste to a more secret haven, deep in the Forest of Arden, where there are 'no clocks and the valley was deep, surrounded by trees, impossible to tell the hour by the sun. The days went slipping by, each one passing in a golden haze.'[36] Their hosts, the Lord and Lady of the forest, with their attendant Robin, deliberately evoke the fairy world of *A Midsummer Night's Dream*, as well as the green world of *As You Like It*, so that Violetta falls asleep on a 'shaded bank, fragrant with thyme and violets', awakening to find her lover beside her. In these two novels Stratford and its countryside is a vulnerable if seductive refuge from the dangers posed by religious and political terrorism; a home that can act only as a temporary frame since the action of both novels moves towards the protagonists' safe return to their place of origin.

The pastoral, paradisiac associations, which cluster around Shakespeare's garden and Stratford more generally, together with New Places's connotations as a safe house, are countered by darker elements in several of the novels, especially those aimed at the older age range. These often focus on the restrictions represented by Puritanism and the violent repression or rebellion of those adhering to Catholicism at a period when religious faith could be a matter of life and death. According to Roberta Trites, there is a distinction in the way death is used in writing for children and how it functions in adolescent novels. While death in children's books often symbolises individuation and separation from the parent in a context of the natural cycle, in adolescent fiction it confronts readers with the need to accept the inevitability of mortality, including their own.[37] Shakespeare's personal history of child loss, as well as the setting in a period of religious conflict and high mortality rates, offer opportunities for writers to explore a theme which is also perceived as central to many of his works, especially *Hamlet. Loving Will Shakespeare* portrays a Stratford thick with suspicion and death, much of it rooted in religion or superstition. At the start of the novel, the demise of Anne's mother from the plague is caused by contagion spread by compulsory church attendance, while the church graveyard becomes a nightmarish place as the dead are disinterred to make space for newly arrived bodies.

> Though my father tried to shield me from the dreadful sight, for many nights my dreams were haunted by what I had seen and by what I imagined. I awoke screaming in terror, my heart pounding, convinced that I, too, would be flung in the charnel house among the bones of the dead while I was still alive and breathing.[38]

Other deaths and dangers follow. Anne's fictional first fiancé, the schoolmaster Edward Stinchcombe, dies in another epidemic, and later her premature half-brother and his father are buried in the same graveyard. Her best friend marries into a recusant Catholic family and returns to the old faith so that 'their path was strewn with danger and perhaps a terrible death if they were found out.'[39] Later, on the verge of spinsterhood, Anne too risks death when threatened with accusations of witchcraft by her stepsister. Her marriage to Will secures her position, placing her safely, if sometimes sadly, as wife and mother in the Shakespeare family house in Henley Street, where growing emotional distance from her husband, symbolised by the open grave of their dead son, ensures that 'for the first time I did not accompany him across the Clopton Bridge when he left for London.'[40] Only Shakespeare's message at the end of the novel, that he has ordered a 'handsome new bed', holds out the possibility that 'all will change' with his return, though for the knowledgeable reader this also serves as a reminder that Shakespeare's own death will follow in a few years' time.[41]

In *Swan Town*, although Stratford sometimes appears as the garden that Shakespeare recalls at the novel's end, full of 'Buttercups, carnations, cowslips, daffodils, daisies, eglantines, harebells, violets, marigolds, lady's-smocks, lilies, and of course the rose'[42] it too is a place haunted by death. Susanna recounts the macabre history of New Place, in which a daughter was poisoned by her father, and excitedly counts the secret rooms it holds, one of which will provide her with privacy in which to write.[43] Later her dead brother appears as a comfortingly homely ghost 'sitting on the chair by my desk.'[44] She also becomes increasingly alert to the ways the town harbours growing intolerance and violence, from the Puritan defacing of the Guild chapel in 1597, to a witchcraft trial and ducking from Clopton Bridge, which prompt her to join ardently in the secret Catholic practices attributed to her family. After Hamnet's death, Susanna is prompted to write her satirical play, *The Celebrated History of the Parrot King*, denouncing England under Elizabeth's rule,[45] a dramatic venture which puts her at risk of arrest and execution as a traitor. A visit by Susanna and her father to Hamnet's grave sets the scene for an important exchange about the mystery of death, which leads them to explore the charnel house with its bones and skulls. While clearly intended primarily as an exploration of the emotional sources for the creation of *Hamlet* in relation to the religious concerns which drive much of the novel, Shakespeare's half-jesting conclusion that 'something is rotten in the town of Stratford'[46] also points forward to the plotting by the Puritan Sir Colin Hill which will threaten the Catholic Shakespeare family, and links the novel's treatment of death with the political and religious setting.

While *Stratford Boys* is generally a more celebratory and comic depiction of a Stratford characterised by community, enterprise and friendship, it too explores some sombre aspects of the town's life, such as the risk of death hovering around Mary Shakespeare's pregnancy late in life or the dangers that cutting a foot on a rusty nail may bring. The rehearsals of Shakespeare's evolving play take place in the churchyard, but since the novel deals with Shakespeare as a boy, the death of Hamnet has no place in the story. Instead intimations of mortality are deepened by the introduction of a dying harper, pining for the spiritual and physical refuge once offered by the dissolved monasteries.

> A hood looked over the churchyard wall. Out of the tail of his eye Adrian saw a sinewy hand wrapped round a staff, a glint of white cheekbones underlining a hollow eye socket in the cavern of the hood, and recognized Death come to claim them, all and some. ... The other

> hand, a branch of ill-knit bones, extended over the wall and pointed. Adrian felt the marrow of his own bones congeal, the sun-warmed stones at his back grow chill. It was a bright balmy evening, they sat among may buds and fragrant vernal grass, the best of the spring before them, but the charnel house was not ten yards away and they all knew what lay beneath the turf where they were sitting. *In the midst of life we are in death.*[47]

This passage is echoed thematically in others about ghosts, purgatory and the proper rites for the dying, presented either as debate or as inner thought processes conveyed through skilful use of free indirect discourse.[48] Together with the initial conceit of the novel, that Shakespeare first began as a playwright by rewriting a mystery play, and the frequent references to the ending of performances of religious play cycles at Coventry and elsewhere, Mark succeeds in linking the cultural and emotional impact of the Protestant Reformation, the persistence of residual Catholic beliefs, with an almost elegiac exploration of mortality.

The Fool's Girl further develops the bittersweet atmosphere of *Twelfth Night,* which opens with actual and supposed deaths of brothers and ends with Malvolio's promise of revenge. Rees's Illyria is a Catholic state which reveres the cup which contained one of the gifts brought to Bethlehem by the Magi, and Malvolio is transformed from Puritan to a Machiavellian Jesuit hoarding holy relics and an arms cache in the Warwickshire manor house owned by Sir Andrew. Although most of the novel's deaths occur outside Stratford, such as the sack of Illyria, the murder of Sir Toby, and Malvolio's own fate in a climactic shoot-out, Trinity Church graveyard is again used as the setting for a scene in which Shakespeare takes flowers to his son's grave, seeks the help of three witch-like figures and also remembers the drowning of a Stratford girl as he mulls over his work on *Hamlet. The Lord of the Dreaming Globe,* on the other hand, treats the churchyard setting with a mix of humour and ghoulish glee, while it is the children who protect Shakespeare, rather than the other way round. In order to escape the spies on watch on every Stratford street corner, Will and Meg devise a plan inspired by *Romeo and Juliet.* Like the heroine of his play, Shakespeare takes a drug that will produce the semblance of death, and is interred in the family vault beside his son's tomb. Before Shakespeare wakes the children discover Marlowe about to kill his rival, but Meg succeeds in persuading the former playwright to abandon his revenge, having learned from performing *Titus Andronicus* the futility of such plots. Unsurprisingly the story ends with the children's safe return to their home in the north, where they relate their adventures to the admiring Marsden elders, and the novel concludes with words taken from the title of a Shakespeare play, *All's Well that Ends Well*.

Such an ending is characteristic of fiction for younger readers. Christopher Clausen differentiates between fictions of home for children and those for young adults.

> When home is a privileged place, exempt from the most serious problems of life and civilization – when home is where we ought, on the whole, to stay – we are probably dealing with a story for children. When home is the chief place from which we must escape, either to grow up or ... to remain innocent, then we are involved in a story for adolescents or adults.[49]

Although neither Anne nor Susanna fully escapes their home they mature through the challenges they meet, and the telling of their own stories. Violetta regains her dukedom and her home, and sees her dead mother's story brought alive in Shakespeare's play. Young Will Shakespeare basks in the applause of his family and friends and begins to plan his next play, not yet knowing that he has started on a path which will take him away from this community. In all these young adult novels Stratford becomes a space in which the meaning and nature of home can be tested and interrogated, most of all through the impact of political and religious ideologies on its supposed security. Although a 'privileged place', fictional Stratford is by no means 'exempt from the most serious problems of life and civilization.'[50] Instead, it intriguingly mirrors some of the dilemmas of our own day, and offers a dynamic location in which to explore how the young find or create their own futures.

Susanne Greenhalgh is Head of Ethics and Interdisciplinary Developments in the Department of Drama, Theatre and Performance at the University of Roehampton, London. She has a particular interest in Shakespearian adaptations and appropriations in literature and the media, and in Shakespeare and the home. Publications include edited essay collections on *Shakespeare and Childhood* (with Kate Chedgzoy and Robert Shaughnessy, CUP 2007) and *Shakespeare and the 'Live' Theatre Broadcast Experience* (with Pascale Aebischer and Laurie Osborne, Bloomsbury 2018), a special edition of *Shakespeare*, commemorating the 200th anniversary of the Lambs' Tales from Shakespeare (with Kate Chedgzoy 2007), and many essays on drama for children, and Shakespeare and his contemporaries on radio and television.

Notes

1. Barbara Hodgdon, 'Stratford's Empire of Shakespeare; Or, Fantasies of Origin, Authorship, and Authenticity: The Museum and the Souvenir', in *The Shakespeare Trade: Performances and Appropriations* (Philadelphia: University of Pennsylvania Press, 1998), 205.
2. Erica Hateley, *Shakespeare in Children's Literature: Gender and Cultural Capital* (London: Routledge, 2009), 81.
3. Hateley, 50.
4. Kate Chedgzoy, 'Shakespeare in the Company of Boys', in *Shakespeare and Childhood*, ed. Kate Chedgzoy, Susanne Greenhalgh and Robert Shaughnessy (Cambridge: Cambridge University Press, 2007), 184.
5. John Bennett, *Master Skylark: a Story of Shakspere's Time* (New York: The Century Company, 1897). The story was originally published as instalments in *St. Nicholas Magazine*.
6. Geoffrey Trease, *Cue for Treason* (Oxford: Blackwell, 1940); Gary Blackwood, *The Shakespeare Stealer* (New York: Dutton, 1998), *Shakespeare's Scribe* (New York: Dutton, 2000), *Shakespeare's Spy* (New York: Dutton, 2003). Pat Pinsent observes that 'the themes found in Trease's novel tend also to figure in several more recent texts. The boy from the country seeking to join a company in London; the lost or stolen manuscript; the danger of plague, which may force companies to leave London and go on tour; the challenge for a boy of playing female parts, together with a girl defying the gender embargo; treasonable acts against the queen – one or more of these is to be found in all the later novels I have examined, other than those which focus on Shakespeare himself as a teen-age boy.' See '"Not for an Age but for all Time": The Depiction of Shakespeare in a Selection of Children's Fiction', *New Review of Children's Literature and Librarianship* 10, 2 (2004), 120.
7. Lucy Waddey, 'Home in Children's Fiction: Three Patterns', *Children's Literature Association Quarterly* 8, 1 (Spring 1983), 13–15.

8. Virginia L. Wolf, 'From the Myth to the Wake of Home: Literary Houses', *Children's Literature* 18 (1990), 66.

9. As Pinsent notes (116) '[t]he relevance of the relationship between real and imagined "history" is made apparent by the fact that ... authors have included prologues or afterwords discussing the "truth" or otherwise of the events of the novels.' Several of the books I discuss make explicit their debt to specific scholars in this way. For a recent overview of London theatre companies' visits to Stratford, see J.R. Mulryne, 'Professional Players in the Guild Hall, Stratford-upon-Avon, 1568–1597', in *Shakespeare Survey 60: Theatres for Shakespeare*, ed. Peter Holland (Cambridge: Cambridge University Press, 2007), 1–22.

10. For a balanced overview of recent writing on Shakespeare and Catholicism see David Bevington, *Shakespeare and Biography* (Oxford: Oxford University Press, 2010), especially Chapter 5, 'Religion'. The title of this article alludes to one of the first revisionist publications in this area, Richard Wilson, *Secret Shakespeare: Studies in Theatre, Religion, and Resistance* (Manchester: Manchester University Press, 2004).

11. See Pinsent, 119.

12. The third novel in Blackwood's series, *Shakespeare's Spy* (2003) also emphasises the religious politics of the period.

13. Helen Hackett, *Shakespeare and Elizabeth: The Making of Two Myths* (Princeton: Princeton University Press, 2009), 234.

14. Naomi Wood, 'Introduction: Children's Literature and Religion', *Children's Literature Association Quarterly* 24, 1 (Spring 1999), 1.

15. Douglas Lanier, *Shakespeare and Modern Popular Culture* (Oxford: Oxford University Press, 2002), 150.

16. Lanier, 150.

17. Terry Deary, *The Lord of the Dreaming Globe* (London: Orion Dolphin, 1998). The 'Horrible Histories' now form the basis for a successful CBBC television series, in which Deary, an actor, also performs. Deary has rewritten some of Shakespeare's plays in a variety of modes in *Top Ten Shakespeare Stories* (New York and London: Scholastic Inc., 1999) and currently has a project to use these as a basis for delivering 'Ten-minute Shakespeare' to children's mobile phones. For the importance of Shakespeare in Deary's work see 'An Introduction to ... Terry Deary', in James Carter, *Talking About Books: Children's authors talk about the craft, creativity and process of writing* (London: Routledge, 1999), 105–129.

18. Carolyn Meyer, *Loving Will Shakespeare* (London and New York: Harcourt Inc., 2006). Meyer is an American writer who has produced a long list of historical romances for teenage girls, several set in the Tudor period.

19. Jan Mark, *Stratford Boys* (London: Hodder, 2003). Mark was English; a former school teacher, she became a full time writer in her thirties, publishing fifty children's books before her sudden death in 2006. Twice a winner of the Carnegie Award, together with several other literary prizes, she is noted for her stylish, pared-down prose, command of contemporary social nuance and generic eclecticism, having produced picture books, short stories and non-fiction, as well as many novels. She also taught creative writing.

20. Michael, J. Ortiz, *Swan Town: The Secret Journal of Susanna Shakespeare* (London and New York: Harper Collins, 2006).

21. She is given the name 'Anne' by Shakespeare.
22. Celia Rees, *The Fool's Girl* (London: Bloomsbury, 2010). Rees is best known for adolescent novels which combine romance and the supernatural in vividly realised historical settings.
23. Mark, 1.
24. Mark, 75–76.
25. Katherine Scheil, 'The Second Best Bed and the Legacy of Anne Hathaway', *Critical Survey* 21, 3 (2009), 41–53.
26. Meyer, 38.
27. Meyer, 261.
28. Meyer, 261.
29. Ortiz, 63.
30. Ortiz, 4.
31. Ortiz, 190.
32. Ortiz, 191.
33. *Richard II*, 2.1.42.
34. Deary, *Dreaming Globe*, 27–28.
35. Rees, *The Fool's Girl*, 241.
36. Rees, 62.
37. Roberta Seelinger Trites, *Disturbing the Universe: Power and Repression in Adolescent Literature* (Iowa City: University of Iowa Press, 2000), 118.
38. Meyer, 10.
39. Meyer, 170.
40. Meyer, 260.
41. Meyer, 1, 262. Meyer's 'Author's Note' records the dates of Shakespeare's and Anne's deaths. On the significance of the bed in accounts of Anne Hathaway see Scheil, 'The Second Best Bed'.
42. Ortiz, 92.
43. Ortiz, 90, 91.
44. Ortiz, 53.
45. Ortiz, 52.
46. Ortiz, 125.
47. Mark, 36.
48. Although *A Midsummer Night's Dream* is clearly referenced in the play rehearsals, the casting of workmen, and the mocking response to the performed play by a local lord and his wedding guests there are also many implicit allusions to *Hamlet*.
49. Christopher Clausen, 'Home and Away in Children's Fiction', *Children's Literature* 10 (1982), 143.
50. Clausen, 143.

Chapter 3

Stratfordian Perambulations

or, Walking with Shakespeare

Julie Sanders

> I bequeath myself to the dirt to grow from the grass I love,
> If you want me again look for me under your boot-soles.
> —Walt Whitman, *Song of Myself*

There has been a recent upsurge of interest in walking both as a social and physiological practice in a range of disciplines stretching from literature to geography, and from anthropology to performance studies. Walking works as an enabler as well as a focus of analysis in discussions about mobility paradigms and phenomenology, giving experientially based access to the kind of subterranean histories of place that have become popular in creative non-fictional writing of late.[1] In her extended study of walking, *Wanderlust*, Rebecca Solnit observes that it is a multidisciplinary engagement: 'The most obvious and the most obscure thing in the world, this walking that wanders so readily into religion, philosophy, landscape, urban policy, anatomy, allegory, heartbreak.'[2] Naturally enough, walking studies

Notes for this section begin on page 51.

also impinge on Shakespearean scholarship and in particular on work relating to Shakespeare-freighted sites such as Stratford-upon-Avon, where the loaded discourses of tourism and personal encounter are predominant in the practical experience of visitors and the subsequent oral or printed account of that experience. For these reasons, this article asks what it might mean, either for the individual or the collective, to 'walk with Shakespeare'.

Phenomenology as a critical practice has gained ground of late in cognate disciplines in the humanities and the social sciences, and cultural geographers such as John Wylie have constructed innovative and deliberately testing academic pieces that are directly structured around walks (for example, Wylie's perambulation of Glastonbury Tor in Somerset).[3] Tim Ingold and Christopher Tilley have long argued from the vantage point of anthropology and archaeology for the intrinsic value of walking sites and recording responses to weather, light, soundscape, vistas and sensory reactions.[4] In the context of performance studies, Mike Pearson has been a pioneer of this kind of hands-on or 'grounded' approach to ideas of place and location.[5] But is any such deep reading possible to produce from a 'Shakespearean' walk when that experience is in itself, especially in Stratford-upon-Avon, always so closely hedged around, and to a certain extent defined, by the demands of local finance and tourism, and, in an even wider sense, by the particular mobilisations of the global brand that is 'Shakespeare'? To what extent can these walks only ever remap and reaffirm the fact that 'Stratford-upon-Avon' as we know it is a tourist industry invention which frequently bears little relation to early modern actuality? Is the 'Shakespeare' that we locate in this place himself already always a construct, a cultural icon fashioned by centuries and communities subsequent to the playwright's own, in order to feed the demands of a national economy and the gross national product by drawing millions of visitors to an otherwise fairly nondescript Midlands market town? Do the texts themselves recede ever further from view in this process so that we find that we may be walking with 'Shakespeare', a cut-out head fashioned to adorn a thousand logos and carrier bags, but not with the complex textual, performative and historical Shakespeares that we might hope or imagine lie at the heart of much academic debate? Where do we even begin to reconcile these multiple versions of the bard? Indeed should we? In the following article, I will pose a series of questions for further analysis around the issues that I think

Stratford-upon-Avon as a site, as both a replicated and reproduced site – and in particular as a walked site – actively mobilises and promotes.

The 'Psychogeography' of Stratford

There is now a recognised canon of theoretical writing on walking as art and action: Walter Benjamin's invocation of the flâneur in *The Arcades Project*; Henri Lefebvre's *The Production of Space* and Michel de Certeau's *The Practice of Everyday Life* among them.[6] This article readily acknowledges the underlying scaffold to its methodology provided both by de Certeau's interest in the relevance of quotidian acts in the production of larger societal meanings and Lefebvre's influential notion of the cultural competencies attached to particular places and sites that are produced by communal practices and understandings of the same.[7] But I also want to suggest that there are particular mobilisations of desire and memory that are at stake when the walking practices involved are associated with a figure as deeply embedded within English literary culture as Shakespeare. In this way, then, place becomes imbricated with person and vice versa, but in turn place becomes enmeshed and entangled with the personal response to both.

Often cited in discussions of walking and art concerned to provide a teleology for their subject are the thoughts, writings and productions of Guy Debord and the Situationists in Paris in the 1960s; their 'subversive walking' led to the body of work now often understood through the label of 'psychogeography'. Paris, London and New York, it might be added, are now the key sites of urban walking literature in the psychogeographic mould; the Lake District in the north of England has perhaps a parallel status in the canon of rural walking, a teleology which finds its alternative roots in English Romanticism. I will attempt here to suggest that both these socio-literary histories of the urban and rural constructions of the art and act of walking have specific relevance for the particular and peculiarly Shakespeare-branded locale of Stratford-upon-Avon and its own self-conscious deployment of walking as social practice and capitalist industry.

Debord famously articulated the notion of the 'drift' or *dérive*, which created walking as an oppositional mode of movement; the Situationists, or at least critical responses to them, emphasised the supposedly liberating and liberated effects of walking without pre-ordained purpose, although I would argue that it is questionable how much any walk already conceived of in terms of artistic practice can be truly without form in this way. In Debord's wake, psycho-geographers claimed to operate without formal maps, although often their walks are subsequently 'mapped' through the act of memory and narrative recording.[8] In an effort to trace much of this interest in pedestrian practice and artistic product to the particular brand and construct of 'Shakespeare', this analysis will focus initially on the phenomenon of organised walks around the idea of the Bard – his works and his life – that are offered and take place, on a daily basis, in Stratford-upon-Avon. The very phrase 'organised' takes us into a realm other than the Situationist one; there are a series of managed expectations and a form of attentive mobility in these instances to which we need to pay heed.[9] Many such walks are collaborative pro-ductions between the local council and local businesses; others are acts of personal entrepreneurship by 'resting' actors in the vicinity and, in this respect, perform an intriguing connection with nightly performances on the official, institutional stages of the Royal Shake-speare Theatre. From this strictly localised vantage point, the focus of this article will broaden to consider a longer distance walk that locates Stratford as its starting point and which, in one studied and self-conscious performance of it, became the basis of a published memoir by the then artistic director of the Globe Theatre in London, Dominic Dromgoole. Both forms of walking in and through place, and in and through Stratford-upon-Avon in particular, will be under-stood within a wider nexus of cultural needs and desires, aesthetic as well as economic, spiritual as well as secular, not least as they circulate around the labile figure of Shakespeare and his works.

Nicola Watson has written suggestively about Stratford's pecu-liar quality as a 'literary shrine' and the way that, as a place, it has encouraged visitors to tread its tourist trails since as far back as the eighteenth century.[10] She quite deliberately invokes the lexicon of 'pilgrimage' to map and understand these social practices across time, although she defines this behaviour in predominantly secu-lar terms: 'the literary pilgrimage takes over much of the language, protocols, and emotional structures of religious pilgrimage'.[11] While Watson's understanding of the ways in which 'places associated with writers' bodies' have in recent times substituted for those associated with saints is acute, I would argue that the spiritual traces nevertheless persist in these performances of so-called 'tourist trails' or geographical itineraries linked to particular writers and their work.[12] The 'bardolatry' oft-invoked by cultural materialists in the 1990s is not necessarily entirely emptied out of spiritual significance in these forms and modes of behaviour. By performing the English landscape and the particular example of Stratford-upon-Avon through designated tourist walks, through the repeated and shared experience of visiting sacred sites, literary or otherwise, centuries-old practices of place, space and faith actually converge in complex ways.[13] From this vantage point, even the specialised, highly localised organised walks taking place in a Midlands market town and tied to highly contemporary notions of tourism and trade can be seen to have tendrils that reach far back into ancient practices.

Today, the only parallel geographical site where official, often commercial, 'Shakespearean walks' proliferate to a similar extent to the phenomenon already noted in Stratford is the city of London, site as it were of those 'other' parts of the Shakespearean biography: the professional playhouse experience as opposed to his birth, childhood, marriage in and eventual retirement back to, the Warwickshire countryside. In this article, with a focus squarely on Stratford as site and concept, I can only gesture to London as an important nodal connective to Stratford on the wider 'Shakespearean map' as it has been drawn by scholars, biographers, practitioners, engaged amateurs and the all-powerful heritage industry alike.

Though Dromgoole's aforementioned walk actually predated the inauguration of an official long-distance path stretching from Stratford to the reconstructed Globe Theatre on the Bankside in the capital, in a sense his self-conscious progress south through the English countryside, which he undertook with his friend Quentin Seddon but published under the rather more individual heading of *Will and Me*, traverses the same desire lines that led to the installation of that formal route on British literary tourism's walking itineraries.[14] Watson writes of the 'emotional affect' of 'doing Stratford' and this same potent mix of tourist practice aligned with acts of personal memory and engagement is embedded in Dromgoole's walk.[15] The back section of *Will and Me* constitutes a detailed account of the walk, but therefore also carefully and instructively counterposes this narrative with Dromgoole's own preceding autobiographical musings, which include memories of theatre-going in Stratford and earlier encounters with the Shakespearean text as both text and effect.

The description in turn gestures towards what effects – emotional, physical, intellectual, and fiscal – literary walking tours of this kind are intended to have, or what they might represent for the individual or indeed the collective in terms of personal and/or communal experience(s).[16]

That the Shakespeare brand is crucial to the local economy of Stratford-upon-Avon has been a given ever since David Garrick and the Memorial Festival first 'performed' the association as part of a touristic and memorialising strategy in 1769. Any tourist (even one with no academic training in the reading, studying or staging of Shakespeare) will be aware of, even attentive, to his 'presence' in the town, in the form of heritage sites (often with entrance fees attached) linked to his life and career, from New Place to Anne Hathaway's cottage, the recently refurbished Royal Shakespeare Memorial Theatre to the Birthplace Trust, the Grammar School and Holy Trinity Church, and significant statuary such as the jester at the end of Henley Street (meant to suggest figures from Lear's Fool and Feste to Trinculo) to that of the bard himself, pensively placed at the water's edge of the symbolic River Avon (connected after all with Shakespearean psychogeography as early as Ben Jonson's description of him as the 'swan of Avon' in the hagiographic poem attached to the First Folio in 1623).[17] Watson speaks of this as an 'exercise in spatialized biography' and certainly Stratford is 'branded' in all kinds of ways by the bard's 'presence', not least in countless gestures to play titles (sometimes mediated through awful puns) that decorate the shop signs and cafe names of the town: 'Othello's'; 'Anne Hathaway's Tea Room'; 'As You Like It', and many more.[18]

It is of note the ways in which the recent architectural reconfiguration of the Memorial Theatre has seen the older theatre encased within a new built environment that encourages innovative practice both of Stratford itself (new sightlines between theatre and church provide one very important act of connection to the kinds of itineraries and 'spatialized biographies' mentioned above) and of the theatre as site of memory and memorial practice, where installations provided by local residents and theatre-goers provide personal and communal accounts of encounters with Shakespeare across time.

Even a Debordian *dérive*, then, around Stratford's environs, mapless and aimless, would necessarily produce some form of Shakespearean 'encounter'. But is this encounter necessarily only unfolding within the commodified context of tourism or is something more essential being hailed or evoked by these constant calls to association with Shakespeare's memory and cultural force? One current Stratford town walk offers the experience of being 'in the bard's shoes' – 'As you walk in Shakespeare's footsteps ...' – and would seem to gesture towards the sense of deep experience that Dromgoole's trek aspires to: 'The land we have been moving through attaches you to nature, links you into an original form of the self ...'.[19] The new tower that forms part of the reconfigured Royal Shakespeare Theatre (itself in fact a throwback to the existence of an unbuilt viewing tower in original blueprints for the twentieth-century theatre) offers those who are willing to pay the entry fee the opportunity to achieve new vistas across Stratford-upon-Avon and to recover some of the pre-Shakespearean medieval layouts of the town. We look down, as it were, on the place as it may have been traversed and practised by Shakespeare himself; an alternative aerial viewpoint or perspective on walking with the bard.

There are claims at least, then, to gaining access to a 'real' experience, something that can be shared across the historical divide with the Warwickshire-born playwright himself: treading in his footsteps, walking where he walked and therefore gaining access somehow to the sites of his inspiration. And yet Shakespeare's plays (unlike those of some of his more urbanised contemporaries such as Richard Brome or Jonson) contain little extended rumination on walking as a social practice. And unlike other contemporaries, Shakespeare did not participate in public, sponsored walks, unlike fellow King's Men actor Will Kemp or King's Men playwright Jonson.[20] For all this suggestion of experiential access of phenomenological encounter, there is the telling strapline at the end of the publicity for the Stratford tour that: 'Customers receive a ticket with 5 tear-off vouchers for specially selected shops, pubs, and restaurants'. The walk is endorsed and advertised by the council and the tourist information office websites. Shakespeare visibly and tangibly helps the Stratford economic wheels go around. There's a strange mix here, then, between claims to the deeply affective or emotional – appeals to the long history of pilgrimage and walking as spiritual endeavour, for example – and a highly commoditised tourist industry. The 'Shakespeare Brand' seems to mobilise both camps often in complicated alliance with each other through enterprises like 'Walking with Shakespeare'.

Walking in Will's Footsteps: from Stratford to London

The complicated mobilisations and performances of Shakespeare discussed in the previous section apply equally to Dominic Drom-goole's memoir, *Will and Me*, as both text and event. Dromgoole was from 2006 to 2016 artistic director of Shakespeare's Globe The-atre in London, having taken over from Mark Rylance. The same year of his appointment he published this memoir, which includes an eighty-page account of his walk, with companion Seddon, from Holy Trinity Church in Stratford to the Globe. The church as Shake-speare's burial site is a deliberately emotive opening move but it is one that the preceding sections of the memoir have prepared read-ers for. Dromgoole talks earlier on in the narrative of a lifetime of walking with Shakespeare; carrying the *Complete Works* on treks: 'on holidays or long walks the fat copy has been carried for an innate sense of direction'.[21] This idea of Shakespeare as personal 'map' or guide is strong in the text and there is a persistent psychologising of Shakespearean 'influence' throughout the work. Dromgoole regu-larly offers the idea of the Bard as therapy, of Shakespeare as healer. An earlier successful non-fiction work in the U.K. was naturalist Richard Mabey's *Nature Cure*, a publication that had as its own sub-text the life and poetry of John Clare, another of English literature's great walkers, and Dromgoole offers a kind of conscious re-visioning of that book as 'Shakespeare Cure'.[22] We learn that both walking and Shakespeare, and sometimes the two together, literally 'saved' Drom-goole's life during a period of recovery following a post-university nervous breakdown, walking a familiar and by implication restora-tive landscape (sometimes with *Complete Works* in hand): 'It put me back together again'.[23] This idea, then, of Shakespeare as map is a very particular kind of cultural and personal cartography. There's a suppressed sense of the Stratford to London walk recounted in the book being prompted by a mid-life crisis: Dromgoole refers to just turning forty and the walk is clearly an opportunity to reflect on his own life as well as Shakespeare's known (and speculative) biography.

The walk commences, then, at Holy Trinity Church, a prime cultural landmark if ever one was needed, proving yet again that many of these 'literary' or heritage-based walks are far from being *dérives* in Debord's or even psychogeography's terms; there is always organisation and ordering involved. One hundred and forty miles will be undertaken over seven days. Dromgoole and Seddon's journey was, as previously noted, undertaken prior to formation of the actual 'Shakespeare Way', a new long-distance path connecting Stratford and London, which was officially launched the same year as the book was published. Dromgoole was, though, heavily involved in the promotion of the path (and by extension his own book), meeting its first official walker, Peter Titchmarsh, at the Globe at the end of his journey to exchange publicly a copy of his memoir with the walker's published account of the 'Way'.

The foundation of the 'Way' has been driven by charitable instincts; Titchmarsh's book is sold on behalf of the Shakespeare Hospice (part of the Macmillan Trust) and the idea is that walkers will organise sponsorship on the charity's behalf. Shakespeare as therapy surfaces in this context also, then, and his woodcut image is part of the Hospice logo, with added 'healing hands' to drive home the point. It may seem hard-edged to state this, but it seems true that all this stands at several stages remove from Shakespeare or Shakespearean texts and performances: the title of Titchmarsh's volume is revealing in this regard: *Shakespeare's Way: A Journey of the Imagination*. As one blogger, Bill Orme, tells us: 'there is little to identify the way that Shakespeare trod except that *it is thought* that he stayed in Oxford at the Crown Inn ...' [italics mine].[24]

What these kinds of walks enable, indeed aim to be a positive prompt or stimulus for, is wild speculation on the relationship between man and milieu, reading into the Warwickshire environment direct inspiration for Shakespeare's poetry and plays.[25] Orme states: 'We can still ask ourselves ... such questions as whether the Rollright Stones were in his mind as the backdrop for *Macbeth*, which beech wood inspired the setting for *A Midsummer Night's Dream* ...'.[26] Geographers would want to dwell on the questionable environmental determinism of this, and literary critics may doubt the compulsion to find biographical causality for everything in the plays, and yet there are links here to recent moves within Shakespearean studies: Jonathan Bate has written eloquently about the 'Deep England' that inspired depictions of the natural world in Shakespeare and how his Warwickshire upbringing was the inspiration for the same (similar reflections, in fact, to the ruminations on 'wild garlic and cow parsley' that Dromgoole indulges in as he walks);[27] and none of this is far from Dromgoole's own determination to read 'apposite' passages from the plays en route – Gertrude's onstage narrative of Ophelia's watery demise from *Hamlet*, for example, as the walking

duo lie down by a riverbank one day.[28] This particular passage reveals
the walkers' 'feeling a current of memory running in the air' as they
read, but whose memory exactly is being mobilised in that quotation
is never clarified.[29] What is the status of this memory? What, indeed,
is the status of the memories and thought associations we are being
asked, invited even, to mobilise on similar walks?

Dromgoole would, I suspect, argue that this impulse to read
Shakespeare into the landscape, to use points on the map as 'sites
of memory' to redeploy Pierre Nora's familiar phrase, is deeply culturally ingrained: 'Shakespeare stains every surface of English life.
He's woven into our history, our most private selves, even our landscape.'[30] Dromgoole and Seddon head southwards from Stratford to
Oxford, climbing up into the Chilterns, descending to the Thames
and Maidenhead, and finally walking the river path to the Globe
itself. On the way they stop to take in the resonant landscape of
the Rollright Stones. If not necessarily the inspiration for *Macbeth*'s
blasted heaths, this sacred circle has now entered the performance
lexicon of Shakespeare through Mark Rylance, Dromgoole's predecessor as Artistic Director of the Globe, whose company Phoebus
Cart staged *The Tempest* there one (wet) summer in the early 1990s.

Dromgoole's companion asks if there is a point to the walk and
the answer the director gives at that stage reasserts a wish to share
Shakespeare's direct experience, to 'walk in his shoes': 'Yes, this is
land he would have crossed, this is the arch of the hills, these clus-
tered buildings are the same villages, these church spires are the
same church spires. There is a point.'[31] There is in the Stratford
passages of the memoir a romantic and idealised sense of the British
countryside's resistance to time that the passages on London are less
able, or less willing, to mobilise; there we get a more familiar narrative of 'grey zones' and post-industrial decline that sounds familiar
for regular readers of British psychogeographer and essayist Iain
Sinclair's perambulatory prose acts.

At other points in the account, Dromgoole seems to want to be
that thing he most despises, the analytical academic; he claims that
the walk's two potent sites, its starting point and its destination,
are suggestive of wider operative binaries in the Shakespearean
biographical narrative: 'the home and the away, the domestic and
the wild, the bourgeois gent and the libertine, Stratford and London
... The connecting tissue is what we have chosen to walk along.'[32]
Dromgoole casts the Stratford to London journey that Shakespeare's

own career trajectory took in heady terms: 'He walked, hitched, and later rode away from that place of clammy actuality towards a great metropolis'; it is a Dick Whittington-esque narrative in which Stratford is personified as sweaty and a bit clinging.[33]

More environmental determinism follows a few pages later: 'The soaring passions that are the sonnets are not Stratford.' Dromgoole tells us, 'The burgeoning love for the beautiful youth traces the pattern of [Shakespeare's] separation from Stratford.'[34] Dromgoole, like many Londoners, has a driving sense of what only London can create; in a text that claims to be about 'connecting tissue', then, the London-centric criticism that has dogged scholarship on Shakespeare and early modern drama is oddly reinforced: 'The vivacity and rococo decoration of Shakespeare's plays comes from his London passions. The understructure comes from the seismic movements of heart that only family, and only Stratford, could bring.'[35] So Stratford for Dromgoole is family and houses, and we might think how this idea, this cultural map, is reinforced by (perhaps even created by?) the walking tours on offer in Stratford today and with which I began this chapter. These tours are a guide to biography, of buildings and those who lived in them, and invariably with Shakespeare that brings us back to family: Mary Arden's House, Hall's Croft, New Place. Dromgoole's memoir makes clear that he grew up with Shakespeare and with seeing the Royal Shakespeare Company at Stratford, so we should not underestimate this sense of direct influence from the provincial town's tourist infrastructure and the legitimised practice of its built environment.

There are, admittedly, moments on the walking tour when Dromgoole feels he is directly re-enacting the actions of the Bard. He and Seddon stay for a night with rich friends, and even this sojourn is justified in Shakespearean terms: 'There is a pleasantly Shakespearean feel to it, a night stopping off with a rich patron on the endless to and fro between Stratford and London, delighting the hosts with some theatre discussion and gossip, and then steaming on.'[36] What's interesting to me, though, is that there is no archival evidence for any of this; even that Shakespeare 'walked' in any sustained or engaged way. As already hinted, the early modern playwright we do know who walked, and who walked partly as performance, and for whom we now have a working map of where he went and who he stayed with, was not Shakespeare but Ben Jonson.[37] But Jonson is not good tourist matter in the same way, nor is he particularly saleable in the subgenre of memoir; no Jonson walks to my knowledge exist (and, to my regret, I have yet to pen 'Big Ben and I').[38]

This is, then, in Dromgoole's own words 'an invented pilgrimage', so what purpose does it serve?[39] In part, I suppose, it functions to explain to Dromgoole the importance and significance of Shakespeare in his own life and career, something he has both embraced and struggled with at times. But not all of us are going to end up as directors at the Globe or even as cynical scholars of Shakespeare and adaptation. So what are these walks intended to 'do' for the majority of those who tread them?

Conclusion

There are ways in which the story that these walks purport to 'tell' and their very existence as part of Stratford's quotidian practices are part of a wider commentary on Shakespeare as cultural icon and as key component in the U.K.'s heritage industry. But the willingness of people to make these walks, some short, some, like Dromgoole's efforts, serious commitments of time, also speak to the equally powerful and exploitable desire of people to 'connect' in some way with Shakespeare. We might wish to see the continuing creation of these walks and the creation of writing and acts of performance around them as part of the wider field of biographical 'writings' on Shakespeare. David Bevington recently published a helpful and detailed survey of the long history of Shakespearean biographical writing as part of the Oxford Shakespeare series, but one 'biography' that he spends little time on is Charles Nicholl's phenomenally successful *The Lodger: Shakespeare on Silver Street*.[40] The shadowy archival mention of Shakespeare that lies at the heart of Nicholl's ruminations and its particular association with the cultural geography of Silver Street was uncovered by pioneering work by scholar Alan Nelson, but what intrigues me most here is how this single archival mention of Shakespeare – in a citation relating to the Mountjoy family case – is the springboard for a book that is otherwise something wholly other:[41] not, in fact, a painstaking reconstruction of the playwright's life from hard archival 'presence', but rather the creation of that 'presence' (and often, suggestively, and more ambiguously, Shakespeare's 'shadow') from the surrounding environments, practices and milieu of his time. It is a method that mimics some recent cultural geographical and psychogeographical writing, such as Iain

Sinclair and Rachel Lichtenstein's *Rodinsky's Room*, but it also connects in suggestive ways with the same impulses that drive the desire to walk 'with' Shakespeare that I have been attempting to think about through the spatial prism of Stratford-upon-Avon in this article.[42]

On these walks, from a partial or even a manipulated and constructed 'encounter' with the Bard, whole worlds are fashioned within people's memory and reading experiences, revealing a psychological desire that goes beyond mere tourism and extends beyond mere commodification into something that might be called 'need'. It is that 'need', that 'desire', that everyone from London publishers to Stratford town councillors seeks to capitalise upon; and it is that 'need' that ensures that these walks continue to represent significant endeavours in a repeating series of personal and collective experiences, however shadowy or tangential their actual connection to the Shakespearean 'life' might be.

Julie Sanders is Professor of English Literature and Drama and Deputy Vice-Chancellor at Newcastle University, UK. She is the author of *The Cultural Geography of Early Modern Drama, 1620–1650* (2011), and co-authored *Ben Jonson's Walk to Scotland* with James Loxley and Anna Groundwater for Cambridge University Press in 2015. She is currently working on a project on craft spaces and maker communities in early modern London.

Notes

1. See, for example, Tim Cresswell, *On the Move: Mobility in the Modern Western World* (London: Routledge, 2006); Tim Ingold and Jo Lee Vergunst (eds), *Ways of Walking: Ethnography and Practice on Foot* (Aldershot: Ashgate, 2008); the published writings of Iain Sinclair, in particular *London Orbital: A Walk around the M25* (London: Penguin, 2003) and *Downriver Or the Vessels of Wrath: a narrative in twelve tales* (London: Penguin, 2004 [1991]); and Robert Macfarlane, *The Wild Places* (London: Granta, 2007). Macfarlane has published a study of paths entitled *The Old Ways: A Journey on Foot* (London: Hamish Hamilton, 2012).
2. Rebecca Solnit, *Wanderlust: A History of Walking* 2nd edn (London: Verso, 2003), 3.
3. John Wylie, 'A Single Day's Walking: Narrating Self and Landscape on the Southwest Coast Path', *Transactions of the Institute of British Geographers*, 30, 2 (2005): 234–247.
4. See Ingold and Vergunst (eds) *Ways of Walking*; and Christopher Tilley, *A Phenomenology of Landscape: Paths, Places, Monuments* (Oxford: Berg, 1994) and *The Materiality of Stone: Explorations in Landscape Phenomenology* (Oxford: Berg, 2004).

5. See, for example, Mike Pearson, *In comes I: Performance, Memory, Landscape* (Exeter: University of Exeter Press, 2006).

6. See, for example, Walter Benjamin, *The Arcades Project* trans. Howard Eiland and Kevin McLaughlin (Cambridge, MA: Belknap, 1999); Michel de Certeau, *The Practice of Everyday Life* trans. Stephen Rendell (Berkeley: University of California Press, 1984); and Henri Lefebvre, *The Production of Space* trans. Donald Nicholson-Smith (Oxford: Blackwell, 1991).

7. See Lefebvre, 30, on spatial practice and levels of competence or knowledge.

8. On psychogeography, see Merlin Coverley, *Psychogeography* (London: Pocket Essentials, 2007).

9. I am grateful to Graham Holderness for the suggestive phrase 'attentive mobility' in his response to an earlier version of this paper given as part of the Shakespeare Association of America seminar on Stratford in Seattle, 2011.

10. Nicola J. Watson, 'Shakespeare on the tourist trail', in *The Cambridge Companion to Shakespeare and Popular Culture*, ed. Robert Shaughnessy (Cambridge: Cambridge University Press, 2007), 199–226 (199).

11. Ibid., 200.

12. Ibid., 200.

13. For a stimulating account of early modern spiritual practice of sites, see Alexandra Walsham, *The Reformation of the Landscape: Religion, Memory and Identity in Early Modern Britain and Ireland* (Oxford: Oxford University Press, 2011).

14. Dominic Dromgoole, *Will and Me: How Shakespeare Took Over My Life* (London: Penguin, 2008). On desire lines as both an architectural and landscape planning practice and as a way of thinking about interdisciplinary academic engagement, see Marjorie Garber, 'Discipline Envy' in her *Academic Instincts* (Princeton: Princeton University Press, 2001).

15. Watson, 201.

16. Huge thanks to seminar organiser Katherine Scheil for sending me this reference following our work together at the 2010 ISC conference on 'The Shakespeare Brand' in which I presented an alternative version of this work focused on a comparison between contemporary walking tours of London and Stratford.

17. For those unfamiliar with the jester statue there is a nice image available for viewing on Flicker at time of writing: http://www.flickr.com/photos/damianward/2294767440/ (last accessed 13 August 2012).

18. Watson, 201.

19. Dromgoole, 228.

20. Kemp, the clown from the King's Men, published an account of his dance between London and Norwich, conducted partly for financial gain, in 1600 under the heading *Nine Daies Wonder* (London, 1600). For an excellent analysis of the multiple impulses for Kemp's journey, see Darryl J. Palmer, *Hospitable Performances: Dramatic Genre and Cultural Practices in Early Modern England* (West Lafayette, Ind: Purdue University Press, 1991). I have written more extensively on the literature of mobility and in particular of urban walking in *The Cultural Geography of Early Modern Drama, 1620–1650* (Cambridge: Cambridge University Press, 2011), 133–77.

21. Dromgoole, ix.

22. Richard Mabey, *Nature Cure* (London: Pimlico, 2006).

23. Dromgoole, 153.

24. http://www.cotswolds.info/places/stratford-upon-avon/shakespeares-way-walk. shtml (last accessed 13 August 2012).

25. We might ask if this is so removed from the 'fictional biography' methodology espoused by Stephen Greenblatt in *Will in the World: How Shakespeare Became Shakespeare* (London: Jonathan Cape, 2004) and see his trenchant attack on Jonathan Bate's 'timidity' in his recent biographical outing on the Bard published in the *New York Review of Books*, 17 December 2009. See also the concluding sentences to this article.

26. http://www.cotswolds.info/places/stratford-upon-avon/shakespeares-way-walk. shtml (last accessed 13 August 2012).

27. See *Soul of the Age: The Life, Mind and World of William Shakespeare* (London: Viking, 2008) and Dromgoole, 218.

28. Dromgoole, 222.

29. Ibid., 222.

30. Ibid., 5. Pierre Nora, *Les lieux de memoires* (Paris: Gallimard, 1984).

31. Dromgoole, 221.

32. Ibid., 218.

33. Ibid., 227.

34. Ibid., 235.

35. Ibid., 221.

36. Ibid., 222.

37. This knowledge is now available to us through a recent manuscript find by James Loxley; reflections on the findings on this text were published by James, Anna Groundwater and myself in *Ben Jonson's Walk to Scotland: An Annotated Edition with Essays* (Cambridge University Press, 2015).

38. Intriguingly, later on, Dromgoole confesses that there is a literary precedent for the walk and for publishing an account – that these walks were often organised on the premise of a publication afterlife is one notable detail about the early seventeenth-century explosion of public walks – in Kemp's *Nine Daies Wonder*, op. cit.

39. Dromgoole, 289.

40. David Bevington, *Shakespeare and Biography* (Oxford: Oxford University Press, 2010); Charles Nicholl, *The Lodger: Shakespeare on Silver Street* (Harmondsworth: Penguin, 2007).

41. Alan H. Nelson 'Calling All (Shakespeare) Biographers!: Or, a Plea for Documentary Discipline', in *Shakespeare, Marlowe, Jonson: New Directions in Biography*, ed. J. R. Mulryne and Takashi Kozuka (Aldershot: Ashgate, 2006), 55–67 (esp. 63).

42. Iain Sinclair and Rachel Lichtenstein, *Rodinsky's Room* (London: Granta, 2000). I owe this connection to Stephen Daniels.

&⁹

Chapter 4

Shakespeare's Church and the Pilgrim Fathers

Commemorating Plymouth Rock in Stratford

Clara Calvo

In 1896, the annual celebration of Shakespeare's birthday acquired the proportions of a major cultural event, amply covered by local, national and international newspapers. 1896 was not a specially commemorative year – it didn't mark any special centenary or half-centenary of the birth or death of the poet – but the arrival in Stratford and prominent presence in the celebrations of both the U.S. Ambassador to the court of Saint James and the U.S. Consul in Birmingham turned Shakespeare's annual birthday ritual into an occasion for what Melanie Hall and Erik Goldstein have called the 'diplomatization of culture'.[1] As the following pages will aim to show, Shakespeare and Stratford played a part in transforming Anglo-American relations, which evolved from open hostility after American Independence and the War of 1812 to diplomatic and military alliance in the course of Queen Victoria's reign.[2] In 1896,

Notes for this section begin on page 69.

the evolution in Anglo-American relations was much concerned with the cultures of commemorating Shakespeare and with making Stratford's Holy Trinity Church an American, not only a Shakespearean, *lieu de mémoire*. The presence of American heritage in Holy Trinity Church illustrates how societies remember through commemorative practices, but it also shows how societies that remember sometimes choose to forget.[3]

In Angela Carter's novel *Wise Children* (1991), the Chance sisters, Dora and Nora, board a transatlantic liner carrying with them an earthenware urn, purpose-built in Stoke-on-Trent, in the shape of Shakespeare's bust.[4] Shakespeare, looking like 'a decapitated doll' (112) in Dora's eyes, is hollow inside – his iconic bald forehead can be lifted up, effectively providing a lid. The interior guards a 'precious gift' sent from England to America: a handful of earth from Stratford-upon-Avon, 'dug out of the grounds of that big theatre', as Dora informs us (113). Dora and Nora travel thus, like Count Dracula, with a box full of earth, and their 'sacred mission' is 'to bear the precious dust to the New World' (113). Once the earth from Stratford has reached America, their 'illegitimate father', the Shakespearean actor turned filmmaker Melchior Hazard, will sprinkle it on the set of a lavish adaptation of *A Midsummer Night's Dream*. The sprinkling is programmed to take place before the shooting begins, consecrating thus the Hollywood studio as holy ground ready to receive Shakespeare.

Angela Carter's novel echoes – and also parodies – the sprinkling of Avon water and earth from Shakespeare's garden on Shakespeare Theatre in Dallas, a replica of the Globe playhouse that could be admired at the Great Texas Fair in 1936.[5] The replica Globe had previously been erected for a mock English village in Chicago's World's Fair (1893), also known as the World's Columbian Exposition, as it was meant to commemorate the 400th anniversary of Christopher Columbus's arrival. Chicago's 'English village' was not the only attempt to recreate Shakespeare's rural England on American soil. In 1916, as part of the Tercentenary celebrations, a replica of the town of Stratford-upon-Avon, England, was contemplated in Boston, Massachusetts. Although the replica village was never built, in 1916 the *New York Times* hoped that it would be finished in time for the celebrations of another tercentenary, as in 1920 Americans would commemorate the landing of the *Mayflower* Pilgrims on Plymouth Rock in 1620.[6]

Boston never achieved its permanent Shakespeare village and the Pilgrim Fathers had no replica of the Birthplace for their tercentenary celebrations, but the association of Stratford with Plymouth Rock and of Shakespeare with democracy recurred during the 1916 celebrations. In Boston, Shakespeare's 1916 Tercentenary was celebrated jointly with the Declaration of Independence not on 23 April but on the Fourth of July.[7] Scenes from *Julius Caesar* were performed on the steps of Boston Public Library. Mayor Curley praised Shakespeare and declared him 'the poet of democracy' and John Murray Gibbon, the Canadian poet and publicist for the Canadian Pacific Railway (CPR), linked Shakespeare with the Pilgrim Fathers and the founding of America's democratic nation.[8]

The desire to recreate Shakespeare's Stratford in the United States has its counterpart in a persistent drive to leave a trace of 'America' in Stratford. The best-known, and more conspicuous, instance of U.S. presence in Shakespeare's birth town is perhaps the Shakespeare Memorial Fountain and Clock Tower, donated by a Philadelphia journalist turned philanthropist, George W. Childs, in 1887. The American Fountain, which still stands today at the top of the town's marketplace, is an example of tandem commemoration, as it celebrates Shakespeare together with Queen Victoria's Jubilee.[9] Like most memorials, it allows the commemorators to memorialise themselves – the joint presence of the lion and the eagle leave no doubt about their iconological significance and Shakespeare thus serves to unite England and America in Stratford.

Phineas T. Barnum failed to purchase the Birthplace when it was auctioned in 1847 and therefore he could not transport it to America, but there are other instances of what Kim Sturgess has called 'the gradual involvement of the American people in the material ownership of Shakespeare'.[10] American money went into the building of the first Shakespeare Memorial Theatre, destroyed by fire on 6 March 1926, and the second Memorial Theatre, which opened on 23 April 1932. Well-known examples of American intervention in Stratford are Harvard House – bought by Chicago millionaire Edward Morris with the help of Marie Corelli at the turn of the twentieth century and donated to Harvard University – and a stained glass window, the Seven Ages of Man window in Holy Trinity Church, inspired by Jacques's well-known speech in *As You Like It* (Illustration 4.1). This famous stained glass window that filters light on Shakespeare's grave was also donated by Childs and has long been an American site of pilgrimage in Stratford, more so since it inspired another famous window at the Folger Shakespeare Library in Washington, DC.[11]

Less conspicuous examples of American presence in Stratford include the stained glass window behind the altar in the Guildhall Chapel, on which John Shakespeare, the playwright's father, is memorialised next to King Edward VI. Both Shakespeare's father and King Edward appear in this window as Stratford benefactors (Illustration 4.2). In one of its lower lights, below Sir Hugh Clopton, who rebuilt the church, and the coat of arms of Thomas Polton, Bishop of Worcester, who dedicated the Chapel, one can read the following inscription: 'In the steadfast belief that the Church of Christ upon earth is one, these two panels are dedicated by the Rev.

Illustration 4.1. Seven Ages of Man window. The Chancel, Holy Trinity Church, Stratford-upon-Avon, UK © John Cheal (Inspired Images)

Robert W. Burns D.D. & the members of the Peachtree Christian Church, Atlanta, Georgia, USA' (Illustration 4.3).[12]

All these examples of U.S. presence in Stratford have something in common: they are the outcome of the generosity of one or several American individuals. By contrast, the stained glass window variously called 'American window', 'New American window' and 'American Memorial window' that covers the south wall of Saint Peter's Chapel, situated in the south transept of Stratford's Holy Trinity Church (Illustration 4.4), bears an inscription boasting to be 'The Gift of America to Shakespeare's Church'.[13]

The stained glass was the work of a well-known Gothic Revival London firm, Heaton, Butler and Bayne. It was erected by the vicar of Trinity Church, Rev. George Arbuthnot, thanks to donations from

Illustration 4.2. King Edward VI and John Shakespeare. Guildhall Chapel, UK.

Illustration 4.3. Dedication panels. Peachtree Christian Church, Atlanta, Georgia, U.S.A.

numerous U.S. citizens. As *The New York Times* explained in 1896, the window was financed 'with money received from American visitors to Shakespeare's tomb and from others whom the vicar interested in the project during a recent visit to the United States.'[14] The window was unveiled by the U.S. Ambassador, Hon. T. F. Bayard, as part of Shakespeare's birthday annual celebration on 23 April 1896, although, at the time, the stained glass was far from being finished. A postcard of the window dating from 1896 shows that only the three central lights had been completed by April 1986 (Illustration 4.5).[15] In spite of this, the window was unveiled, attracting considerable media attention.[16] The 1896 celebration of Shakespeare's birthday, in fact, was marked by American interests. Together with the unveiling of the new American window in Holy Trinity Church, a portrait of

Illustration 4.4. The New American window, St. Peter's Chapel © John Cheal (Inspired Images).

Edwin Booth was presented by G. F. Parker, U.S. consul in Birmingham, on behalf of The Players Club of New York, to the Shakespeare Memorial Theatre and Museum. The previous night, at the dinner of the Birmingham Dramatic and Literary Society, Parker, as its president, read a letter sent by President Cleveland.

The cultural biography of this window links the ritual remembrance of Shakespeare and the presence of U.S. visitors as literary tourists in Stratford. The ceremony of its unveiling and the circumstances that surrounded it, including the speeches, the prayer of dedication and the extensive media coverage are part of the substructures of Anglo-American diplomacy before the First World War. The cultural life of this window equally shows that what Nicola Watson

Illustration 4.5. The New American window in 1896. © The Francis Frith Collection.

has called 'the thrills of literary tourism' are often inseparable from the assertion of national identity and may contain a measure of political friction.[17] The fact that the window was officially dedicated before it was completed poses additional questions, such as why it was felt necessary to unveil it in 1896. Financial reasons were no doubt powerful, as, once unveiled, the window itself would encourage further contributions towards the cost of completing it – 1896 was also the year in which the Birthplace established an admission charge, initially fixed at sixpence.[18] Arbuthnot's decision to charge an admission fee to Shakespeare's Church was objected to in the U.S., and the window was part of extensive rebuilding undergone by Holy Trinity Church in the late 1880s, some of which was not generally applauded, to the extent that the Vicar was labelled a 'second Gastrell'.[19]

The American Memorial window consists of five upper and five lower lights crowned by a rose or wheel window. It contains a complex iconographical display, arranged around a central axis occupied by the Incarnation, or Madonna with child, in the upper light and the Epiphany, or Adoration of the Magi, in the lower light. On either side of Mary and Jesus, a series of eminent figures appear in the upper lights, and the lower lights are dedicated to several narrative scenes. Upper and lower lights are thematically linked. Most of the figures depicted in the upper lights bear relation to the Anglican Church, to Stratford or to America (Illustration 4.6).

On the left, the English notables are Saint Wulfstan, Bishop of Worcester, who symbolises the continuity between Anglo-Saxon and Norman Christianity, and John of Stratford, the founder of Holy Trinity Church. Next to them stands King Charles I with Saint Egwin, Bishop of Worcester, who built the Abbey at Evesham and William Laud, Archbishop of Canterbury. On the right, William Penn, the founder of Pennsylvania, holding a copy of his book *No Cross No Crown*, written during his imprisonment in the Tower of London in 1668, keeps company with Amerigo Vespucci and Christopher Columbus.[20] To their right, Bishop Eric of Greenland, the first bishop beyond the Atlantic, stands next to Samuel Seabury, Bishop of Connecticut and the first Bishop of the American Episcopal Church.

Illustration 4.6. The New American window. Upper Lights. © John Cheal (Inspired Images).

Each of the lower lights (Illustration 4.7) is closely related to its corresponding upper light. From left to right (and excluding the central lower light that contains the adoration of the Magi), they illustrate the building of the South aisle of Holy Trinity Church under John of Stratford, the execution of Archbishop Laud, the Landing of the Pilgrim Fathers on Plymouth Rock and the consecration of Bishop Seabury in Aberdeen in 1787.

If read from left to right, these four narratives display an attempt to establish an historical continuity from the building of Holy Trinity to the origins of the American Episcopalian Church. In Foucaultian terms, this attempt is more a genealogy than a history, full of fractures and 'the singularity of events', despite its evident inclination for 'origins' and a linear conception of the past.[21] The vicar of Holy Trinity Church, Rev. Arburthnot, had a powerful reason to include Bishop Seabury in the window, not only for his pioneering role in the American Episcopalian Church but also for the benefits involved in strengthening his connection to Holy Trinity Church. As he explains in his guide to Shakespeare's Church:

> ... attention should be directed, especially on the part of Americans, to a copy of the Agreement drawn up between Bishop Seabury and his consecrators, which is hung up in the Church for their inspection. It contains one clause to the effect that the Episcopal Church in Connecticut is to be in full communion with the Episcopal Church in Scotland; and appears of such interest to American Church people that it has been printed, and a copy can be obtained from the Custodian of the Church for twopence, any profits from the sale going to the adornment of the American Chapel in the South Transept.[22]

Illustration 4.7. The New American window. Lower Lights. © John Cheal (Inspired Images).

Scotland, then, not England, is the link between American and British Episcopalian Churches, so Arbuthnot's appropriation of Seabury for the American window is one of the fractures in the genealogy linking Shakespeare's Church and America.

The unveiling of the window in 1896 was a highly theatrical affair.[23] The U.S. Ambassador arrived in Stratford from Birmingham by the Great Western Railway, with the U.S. Consul, G. F. Parker. After being met at the station by the Rev. Arbuthnot and the Mayor, Mr Smallwood, they drove off in open carriages to the church while the crowds watched and cheered. The service in Holy Trinity Church included several hymns and two speeches by Arbuthnot and Bayard. Arbuthnot spoke first while the window was still covered by a white cloth, describing the stained glass in detail before it could be seen. Bayard then pulled the cord and the white cloth came down, revealing the unfinished window.

In his speech, Rev. Arbuthnot explained that the window aimed to show how 'the Old World and the New were united in the adoration of the Incarnate Christ' and its purpose was to carry 'a message of peace and goodwill.'[24] In 1896, this message was hardly there. When the window was unveiled, visitors could only see the three central upper and lower lights, which rather than peace seem to encode ideological friction. If the window celebrates the union of the Old World and the New, and the union of their Episcopalian churches, it is surprising that it chooses to memorialise such a large number of 'martyrs' and 'dissenters': Charles I, William Laud, William Penn and the Pilgrim Fathers (Illustration 4.8).

If the aim of the window is to praise concord and religious tolerance, the presence of Charles I and Bishop William Laud next to the Pilgrim Fathers praying on Plymouth Rock after alighting from the *Mayflower* undermines its message. To see Charles I commemorated as 'martyr' next to the Mayflower Pilgrims presented as heroic freedom fighters giving thanks to God because they managed to escape Stuart tyranny is odd.[25] The choice of the Pilgrim Fathers in a stained glass window that intends to strengthen the bonds between England and the U.S. only works if history is remembered selectively. The *Mayflower* and the Pilgrim Fathers are the iconic representation of a myth of origin linking England and America. Plymouth Rock symbolises freedom, republicanism and the promise of religious tolerance, i.e., the lucky escape of the Pilgrims from the land of religious intolerance that was Shakespeare's England. For the joint commem-

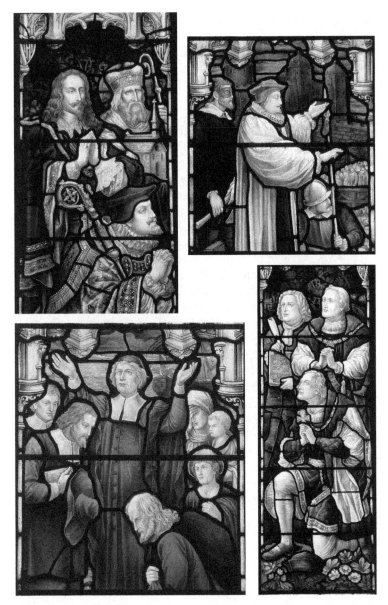

Illustration 4.8. Martyrs and Dissenters: Charles I, William Laud, William Penn and the Pilgrim Fathers. © John Cheal (Inspired Images).

to work, it is necessary to achieve a convenient erasure of unwanted historical detail from collective memory. As Paul Connerton reminds us, communities remember selectively and modernity knows how to forget.[26] The lack of evidence of any link between Shakespeare and the *Mayflower*, the Pilgrim Fathers or early seventeenth-century New Englanders, such as Cotton Mather, is often conveniently forgotten or bypassed in attempts to establish links that relate the plays to the earliest colonists.[27] As an American *lieu de mémoire*, the American Memorial window provides the literary tourist with a puzzling experience. The presence of Plymouth Rock on the stained glass window of Shakespeare's Church is an unsettling sight, given that the Pilgrims who landed there were escaping precisely from what Holy Trinity Church stood for.

The greatest act of erasure of collective memory is perhaps the attempt made by Rev. Arbuthnot to justify the presence of Charles I on the American window in his speech on 23 April 1896: 'The propriety of introducing King Charles and Laud is apparent when it is remembered that they came immediately after Shakespeare's time, and saw the rise and development of the Puritans, who had so much to do with colonising America'.[28] In a previous phase, the design of the window was going to depict Charles I's beheading, instead of William Laud's execution. If the original design had been carried out, the window would have encoded, even more explicitly, the tension between monarchy and republic that makes the U.S. different from Britain – and which was amply referred to in his speeches by the U.S. Ambassador, Mr Bayard. For Bayard, 'Shakespeare was a common bond of feeling and sympathy and admiration between the two great families of the English speaking people', but, as he added, 'Those who made their home in lands beyond the seas had chosen for themselves a different framework of society, having exchanged a Monarchy for a Republic'.[29] At the luncheon served in the town hall after the service, the U.S. Ambassador rose after the toasts to claim that 'Shakespeare was as good an American as he was an Englishman' and struggling to reconcile the assertion of national identity with the appropriation of Shakespeare as 'the poet of the English speaking race', Mr Bayard declared himself 'a Republican citizen but a subject of King Shakespeare'.[30]

The religious and political frictions that the American Memorial window addresses add to another element of tension in a window dedicated not to Shakespeare but to Shakespeare's Church. On 23 April 1896, when the cord was pulled and the window revealed,

Rev. Arbuthnot said the prayer of dedication: 'In the name of the Father, and of the Son, and of the Holy Ghost, we bless and dedicate this window erected in the faith of Jesus Christ, and as a memorial of his servant, William Shakespeare. Amen'. In what sense the American Memorial window is a memorial to Shakespeare is not self-evident. A literary tourist that scans the window for references to Shakespeare will be hard-pressed to find a connection with the playwright or his works beyond his name at the bottom of the fourth lower light. Shakespeare's iconic image is not found amongst those who link England and America. On the First World War Memorial in a stained glass window at the old college hall of the University of Canterbury, New Zealand, Shakespeare stands next to Chaucer to represent the forces of civilisation, while First World War soldiers repel the attack of demon-like invaders. On the window unveiled on his birthday in 1896 in Stratford, Shakespeare is only memorialised though the association of his name with Holy Trinity Church.

In order to read the American Memorial window as a memorial to Shakespeare, one has to recall the 400 dollars from American visitors to Shakespeare's grave that contributed to the cost of erecting it. The gift of America to Shakespeare's Church is also the gift of Shakespeare's Church to America, as it served to build a memorial to the founding myth of the U.S. – the quest for religious and political freedom – while at the same time, construing a link between the U.S. and Britain, through the Episcopalian Church and Shakespeare as the poet of the English-speaking world. Rev. Arbuthnot's memorial window created a new *lieu de mémoire*, a new site of pilgrimage for U.S. tourists, and a new reason for American visitors to visit Shakespeare's Church, showing thus the circularity of cultural practices.

In *Wise Children*, the handful of English soil from the Shakespeare Memorial Theatre never makes it to the set of the Hollywood adaptation of *A Midsummer Night's Dream*. When the occasion arrives, the Chance sisters find out that the sacred earth was defiled by a Persian cat during the railway journey from New York to California. For the duration of the shooting, Nora and Dora stay at a motel called the Forest of Arden, and they quickly find a way to replace the desecrated relic with earth just as meaningful: 'We filled the casket up again with soil from the Forest of Arden, from the facsimile Elizabethan knot garden itself; we thought that would make it more authentic. So there was sacred earth, as good as new'. (129). It is, then, American soil that Melchior Hazard scatters on the set before he gives it its benediction with two raised fingers (137), in a ceremony that rewrites Shakespeare's last speech for Puck and Oberon and recalls, somehow, Garrick's Jubilee. Just as Stratford was absent from and somehow present in the earth the twins used to refill the casket destined to commemorate the playwright's birthplace, Shakespeare is also simultaneously absent and present in the memorial window paid for by Americans to honour his memory.

The presence of Americans and American interests in Stratford-upon-Avon, England, stretches thus beyond the American Fountain in Market Square. The bond between America and Stratford, mostly forged by Victorian and Edwardian visitors and benefactors, rests on contradictory, ambivalent symbols and, as so often happens in rites of remembrance in which the commemorators often commemorate themselves, American presence in Stratford celebrates Shakespeare and asserts national myths and identity at the same time. American commemoration of Shakespeare in Stratford works in two opposite directions, strengthening bonds with Shakespeare's England while simultaneously asserting self-determination and memorialising independence from the nation that gave birth to Shakespeare. The outcome of this double commemorative practice is that Plymouth Rock, the Pilgrim Fathers and the *Mayflower* return to England via the commemoration and memorialisation of Shakespeare. One of Stratford's iconic tourist destinations, Holy Trinity Church, and Plymouth Rock are jointly construed as sites of memory and symbols of origin, tightly linked in the commemorative imagination.

Clara Calvo is Professor of English Studies at the University of Murcia (Spain). Her research interests include the afterlives of Shakespeare and Jane Austen, literary adaptation and cultural memory. She is the author of *Power Relations and Fool-Master Discourse in Shakespeare* (1991) and has co-authored, with Jean-Jacques Weber, *The Literature Workbook* (Routledge, 1998). With Ton Hoenselaars, she has edited *European Shakespeares* (*The Shakespearean International Yearbook*, 8, 2008) and a special issue of *Critical Survey* on *Shakespeare and the Cultures of Commemoration* (2011). She has also edited *The Spanish Tragedy* for the Arden Early Modern Series with Jesús Tronch (2013) and *Celebrating Shakespeare: Commemoration and Cultural Memory* (CUP, 2015) with Coppélia Kahn.

Notes

Research for this paper was possible thanks to Research Project FFI2011-24347, 'Shakespeare and the Cultures of Commemoration II: Remembering Shakespeare', financed by the Spanish Research Agency MEC-ANEP.

1. Melanie Hall and Erick Goldstein, 'Writers, the Clergy, and the 'Diplomatization' of Culture: Sub-Structures of Anglo-American Diplomacy, 1820–1914', in *On the Fringes of Diplomacy: Influences on British Foreign Policy, 1800–194*, ed. John Fisher (Aldershot: Ashgate, 2011).

2. Kim C. Sturgess has shown how the early anti-English sentiment which arrived in the New World with the Puritans gradually gave way to the American appropriation of Shakespeare. See *Shakespeare and the American Nation* (Cambridge: Cambridge University Press, 2004), 26 and *passim*.

3. Paul Connerton, *How Societies Remember* (Cambridge: Cambridge University Press, 1989); *How Modernity Forgets* (Cambridge: Cambridge University Press, 2009).

4. Angela Carter, *Wise Children* (London: Chatto and Windus, 1991).

5. Graham Holderness, 'Bardolatry: The cultural materialist's guide to Stratford-upon-Avon', *The Shakespeare Myth* (Manchester: Manchester University Press, 1992), 2–15, p. 2.

6. *The New York Times*, 25 June 1916.

7. Shakespeare and the Declaration of Independence have a history of joint commemoration. In his will, actor Edwin Forrest specified that annual commemorative rituals would take place on 23 April and 4 July in his home for elderly or disabled actors. See Sturgess, *Shakespeare and the American Nation*, 133.

8. *Boston Herald*, 5 July 1916, front page.

9. Childs also donated memorial windows to William Cowper and George Herbert (Westminster Abbey), and to John Milton (St. Margaret's Church, Westminster). For the dedication ceremony of the American Fountain, see Sturgess, *Shakespeare and the American Nation*, 187–88.

10. *Shakespeare and the American Nation*, 182. See pp. 181–86 for a discussion of Barnum's failed attempt to buy the Birthplace and Mark Twain's use of this anecdote in a letter to raise funds for the Memorial Theatre. See also Louis Marder, *His Exits and His Entrances: The Story of Shakespeare's Reputation* (Philadelphia and New York: Lippincott, 1963), 243–44.

11. James G. McManaway, 'The Folger Shakespeare Library,' *Shakespeare Survey*, 1 (1948), 58–59. The window is located at the west end of the Gail Kern Paster Reading Room and is reproduced in http://www.folger.edu/imgdtl.cfm?imageid=777&cid=1333 (last accessed 14 September 2012).

12. The Peachtree Christian Church, founded in 1925, survives to this day in Atlanta. I owe this information to Christy Desmet.

13. The inscription is preceded by the acronym AMDG (*ad maiorem dei gloriam*).

14. *The New York Times*, 24 April 1896. As the visitors' books kept in the Shakespeare Birthplace Trust Library show, from June 1891 to August 1917, American visitors signed in a separate book.

15. Shakespeare Birthplace Trust Library and Archive (Ref. No. SC10/1/37268).

16. *The New York Times*, 24 April 1896.

17. Nicola Watson, *The Literary Tourist* (London: Palgrave, 2006), 17.

18. Marder, *His Exits and His Entrances*, 245.

19. 'Vandalism at Stratford-upon-Avon', *Shakespeariana*, vol. 7, January 1890, pp.40–44; p.44. Christy Desmet alerted me to criticisms of Arbuthnot's decision to charge an admission fee and of his handling of restoration activity in the Church in *Shakespeariana*, the journal of the Shakespeare Society of New York, edited by Charlotte Endymion Porter. The journal alerted its readers to the new admission charge of 6d for visitors to Trinity Church (vol. 6, November 1889, p. 494) and discussed the restoration process in several editorials, letters to the editor, and excerpts from the Stratford-upon-Avon *Herald* (including vol. 6, October 1889, pp. 459–60; vol. 6, November 1889, pp. 492–6 and pp. 502–506). One of these editorials (vol. 6, pp. 459–60) quotes a sermon by Arbuthnot in which he re-assures his congregation that the restorations are being handled by some of the best architects in England. The editorial objects to these 'improvements' that will transform the church into something very different from the church Shakespeare knew. In another editorial (vol. 6, p. 502) readers are warned that the 'six-penny tax' that the Vicar has imposed on American visitors will be used to pay for those restorations that lovers of Shakespeare may not approve of. Criticism of the building repairs in Trinity Church had already been given attention in *Shakespeariana*, vol. 5, March 1888, pp. 145–7 which reprinted part of a letter to the editor by J.O. Halliwell-Phillipps published in *The Times* (30 January 1888). Behind the accussations against Arbuthnot contained in these editorials and letters there is a concern about the destruction of historical and artistic heritage which, as far as is connected to Shakespeare, also belongs to Americans. Hence the comparison with Francis Gastrell, the eighteenth-century owner of New Place who cut down the mulberry tree and pulled down Shakespeare's house.

20. William Penn is known to have owned Shakespeare's plays, but they remained in England when he travelled to America. Penn's secretary, though, had a copy of Rowe's edition. See Marder, *His Exits and His Entrances*, 296.

21. Michel Foucault, 'Nietzsche, Genealogy, History', in *Language, Counter-Memory, Practice: Selected Essays and Interviews*, ed. Donald F. Bouchard, trans. Donald F. Bouchard and Sherry Simon (Ithaca, NY: Cornell University Press, 1977), 139–64.

22. George Arbuthnot, *A Guide to the Collegiate Church of Stratford-on-Avon*, 10.

23. *Birmingham Daily Post*, 24 April 1896.

24. Ibid.

25. As Sturgess notes, after the Restoration, signatories of Charles I's death warrant were hidden by Puritans and found refuge in New England. See *Shakespeare and the American Nation*, 26.

26. Connerton, *How Societies Remember; How Modernity Forgets*.

27. The supposition that Cotton Mather may have owned a copy of the First Folio is now dispelled, as it has been shown to have originated in a family myth. See William H. Scheide, 'The Earliest First Folio in America?', *Shakespeare Quarterly* 27 (1976): 323–33 and Sturgess, *Shakespeare and the American Nation*, 123.

28. *Birmingham Daily Post*, 24 April 1896.

29. Ibid.

30. Ibid.

Chapter 5

Importing Stratford

Katherine Scheil

In 1886, the American critic William Winter remarked, 'Every pilgrim to Stratford knows beforehand, in a general way, what he will there behold. Copious and frequent description of its Shakespearean associations have made the place familiar to all the world'.[1] But does every pilgrim know the same things about Stratford? How has Stratford's relationship with Shakespeare shifted over time and geography? In what ways has Stratford been 'familiar to all the world', and how have various meanings of Stratford been mobilised in specific times and places? In order to explore these questions, this chapter considers the phenomenon of 'importing Stratford' – that is, non-Warwickshire cities and towns that have taken the name of Stratford for their locale, often with other accessories such as a River Avon or streets named after Shakespearean characters.

To those of us in the twenty-first century, the name 'Stratford' most likely calls to mind the Shakespeare tourist trade in its many forms: Shakespeare's Birthplace, Anne Hathaway's Cottage, the home of the Royal Shakespeare Company and the overall pastoral

Notes for this section begin on page 83.

image of 'Shakespeare Country' in Warwickshire. Many of these aspects, however, are relatively recent developments of the last century and a half. The Shakespeare Birthplace, for example, was not purchased by the Shakespeare Birthplace Trust until 1847 (when the latter was formed). By the 1864 Tercentenary, Shakespeare's birthplace had been 'aggressively restored to Tudor picturesqueness' and Nash House and New Place were purchased that same year. Anne Hathaway's Cottage was a later acquisition (1892), as was Mary Arden's house (1930).[2] Given this history, why have citizens around the world chosen 'Stratford' as a name for their locale, what connotations were they hoping to evoke and how has the choice of this place name shaped the development of the space?[3] If we take into account Tim Cresswell's point that place is 'not just a thing in the world but a way of understanding the world', how have the various associations of 'Stratford' resonated across time in different parts of the world?[4]

The Earliest Stratfords

The two earliest Stratfords predate the evolution of the U.K. Stratford as a tourist destination, and offer evidence for the ways in which ideas of 'Stratford' circulated in colonial North America. Stratford, Connecticut was the first to import the place name in the 1630s, well before the Shakespeare tourist trade developed. The William Beardsley family, one of the founding families of the town, was originally from Stratford-upon-Avon, and 'claimed the honor of securing to the town of Stratford, Conn., its name, in honor of their old native place in their mother country, with much credible evidence'.[5] Although a reference as early as 1630 described Stratford, U.K. as 'a town most remarkable for the birth of famous William Shakespeare', there was little evidence of the Shakespeare tourist trade at the time.[6] According to Roger Pringle, even by the end of the seventeenth century 'there was still little known about Shakespeare even among the well educated ... no biography, not even a short memoir, was available in print to give an account of the dramatist's career and his family background, and thereby generate among some of its readers a curiosity to visit the places connected with him'.[7] In colonial America, Stratford did not yet imply 'Shakespeare', but rather invoked associations of its early settlers' origins.

Over a hundred years later, the second Stratford, in New Hampshire, was chartered in 1773, named after both Stratford, Connecticut and Stratford-upon-Avon, U.K. Many of the settlers had emigrated from Woodbury and Stratford, Connecticut, so their choice of place name had a dual purpose – to hearken back to their Connecticut roots, but also to invoke the growing Shakespearean associations of the U.K. town.[8] Over the course of the later eighteenth century, the Warwickshire Stratford had become well-known as a Shakespearean destination in England. Roger Pringle records that even before Garrick's 1769 Stratford Jubilee, tourist interest had developed at the birthplace, and 'the town generally was wakening to the realization that it had produced a remarkable son, the protection and honouring of whose memory was a matter of civic pride, and even cash'.[9] By 1759, Reverend Francis Gastrell, then owner of New Place, had become so exasperated with the glut of tourists that he infamously had New Place torn down. It is thus no surprise that this second Stratford in New Hampshire took advantage of the early stirrings of the Shakespeare trade. In the early nineteenth century, for those outside of England, Washington Irving's 'Sketch Book' (1819–20), reprinted numerously in England and America, was essential in establishing the global identity of Stratford. Even though Irving described the Birthplace in 1820 as 'squalid', run by a 'garrulous old lady in a frosty red face',[10] his 'Sketch' nevertheless served as the unofficial 'guidebook for American pilgrims arriving in Stratford', including P. T. Barnum, who was inspired to attempt to buy Shakespeare's Birthplace and import it to America.[11]

Around 1832, the third Stratford, in Ontario, was planned along the Little Thames River. The Canada Company wanted their developing town to 'have a strong English connection as did the two towns it had previously established – Guelph (for the royal family) and Goderick (for the British prime minister)', and thus Stratford was a logical choice. To further establish a sense of place, the name of the Little Thames River was changed to the Avon, and the Shakespeare Inn was established in 1832, though it was destroyed by fire in 1849. According to one history of Stratford, Ontario, 'little did they realize that the name itself would set the stage for future benefits'.[12] The choice of Stratford as the town name led to further Shakespeare-related developments: the Stratford Festival (discussed later in this chapter), twelve streets named after Shakespeare characters, an Anne Hathaway park and appropriate names for all ten of the public schools (Shakespeare, Anne Hathaway, Avon, Falstaff, King Lear, Hamlet, Romeo, Juliet, Portia and Bedford).[13] A nearby town was also renamed 'Shakespeare' (previously called Bell's Corners) because of its proximity to the Avon River (which was previously renamed from the Little Thames River).[14] Although the town name was inspired by its English connotations, Stratford, Ontario did not fully develop its associations with Shakespeare until the middle of the twentieth century, with the establishment of the Stratford Festival in 1953. Following Stratford, Ontario, the gradual development of Stratford, U.K. as a tourist site throughout the later nineteenth century led to a boom of satellite Stratfords around the world.

In the latter part of the nineteenth century, the sale of Shakespeare's Birthplace in 1847 helped advertise Shakespeare's Stratford associations, while Stratford expanded as a tourist destination, due in part to a connection with the rail network in 1860 and the restoration of the Birthplace for the 1864 Tercentenary.[15] Americans in particular began to visit Stratford in significant numbers; American travellers were described in an 1868 account as 'the head pilgrims ... with whom it is almost a religion to worship at the shrine of the "Anglo-Saxon" poet', and by 1887, Henry Irving called Stratford 'a Mecca of American pilgrims'.[16] In fact, in a recent study Peter Rawlings credits Americans with 'the invention of Stratford-upon-Avon'.[17] In addition to literati, many ordinary Americans travelled to Stratford around the fin de siècle. Meetings of the Eugene, Oregon Shakespeare Club, for example, often included reports on Stratford 'by some member recently returned from the Shakespeare country'. Starting in 1920, the club history lists as many as eleven women travellers, including one 'who has made frequent visits to Stratford'.[18] The American journal *Shakespeariana*, published in the 1890s, regularly included essays, pictures and articles about Stratford. Thus, it is no surprise to see numerous Stratfords located in America and elsewhere at the end of the nineteenth century, although the connections of these Stratfords with Shakespeare seem to have been less important than the sense of Englishness implied by the place name.[19]

The Tercentenary and the Surge of Stratfords

In the last few decades of the nineteenth century, at least four Strat-fords were established around the world. Stratford, Iowa, founded in 1881, was initially platted by the Western Town Lot Company, the real estate division of Toledo and Northwestern Railroad. When railroad engineer John I. Blair held a meeting of crew members to rename what was currently called 'Rosstown', one crew member sug-gested 'Stratford', after Stratford, Pennsylvania, which was named after Stratford, U.K.[20] The absence of a river in the town was rectified by naming a street 'Avon Street'. The rationale for invoking 'Strat-ford' in rural Iowa seems to have had little to do with the Shake-speare tourist industry or with the ritualistic sense of pilgrimage discussed by scholars such as Péter Dávidházi, but instead aimed to suggest a sense of place and a desire to impart a history to a locale devoid of a past.[21] By this time, it seems that 'Stratford' had evolved into a complex set of meanings and connotations in America, some-times connected to Shakespeare and at other times derived from more general conceptions of pastoral England.

Some American Stratfords, like the one in Iowa, were frontier towns newly settled with the progress of the railroad system. In con-nection with such changes, David Thelen has argued that 'people have resisted rapid, alien, and imposed change by creating mem-ories of a past that was unchanging, incorruptible, and harmoni-ous'.[22] Nineteenth-century Stratford, to many Americans, embod-ied this sense of an 'unchanging, incorruptible, and harmonious' place. Henry James's essay 'In Warwickshire', published in 1877, for example, describes the Stratford area as 'unaltered' and 'a sur-vival from an earlier England'. Even the sheep were 'poetic, historic, romantic sheep' there for 'their presence and their compositional value'.[23] Invoking the stability and order associated with 'Stratford' thus speaks to what Samuel Schoenbaum calls 'Stratfordolatry', where 'the very name Stratford-upon-Avon takes on the glamour of a remote past, conjuring up the English settlement at the *ford* where the Roman *street* crossed the river called by the Welsh *afon*'.[24] Choos-ing 'Stratford' as a name for a newly developed town (like the one in Iowa) seems also to have been in line with the sentiments expressed by Nathaniel Hawthorne in his essay on Stratford: 'To an American there is a kind of sanctity even in an English turnip-field, when he thinks how long that small square of ground has been known and recognized as a possession, transmitted from father to son, trodden often by memorable feet, and utterly redeemed from savagery by old acquaintanceship with civilized eyes'.[25] The concept of 'Stratford' was thus a way to give a history and longevity to a previously nameless place, but the associations of these various Stratfords with Shakespeare had a more variable relationship.[26]

Rather than a completely Shakespeare-centred town, Stratford, Iowa resembles a literary anthology, with streets named after English authors (Goldsmith, Milton, Tennyson, Dryden, Byron, Burns, Moore), suggestive of a broadly cultured place. Shakespeare Avenue is the major north–south street, running to the train depot, figuratively anchoring the other literary place names. Despite the bookish inclinations of the town planners, the history of Stratford, Iowa includes surprisingly few instances in which Shakespeare is invoked. Even so, aside from its status as a literary curiosity, Stratford, Iowa can tell us several important things about how ideas about 'Stratford' circulated. The name of the town, originating in the railroad engineers who platted the city, is indicative of the general knowledge of Shakespeare and the connotations of 'Stratford' among ordinary nineteenth-century Americans – not east coast literati, but rather those who shaped the American frontier.[27]

A second American Stratford appeared around the same time as the one in Iowa, also founded by railroad developers. On the east coast of the United States, Stratford, New Jersey began as a village called 'White Horse' in 1695, named after the White Horse Tavern. During the Revolutionary War, White Horse was an important site for American pirates to transport their booty from the shore to other nearby towns. In the early nineteenth century, the stage coach and railroad brought more population to the area, including developer Charles S. King, who in 1888/89 'saw the possibility of creating a pleasant and ideal community out of the farm land owned by Jacob Lippincott'. King formed the Rural Land Improvement Company and chose the name of Stratford for the name of the new community.[28] By donning a new name and identity, and rejecting its Revolutionary War history, Stratford, New Jersey resembles its namesake in Iowa (founded the same decade) in its desire to evoke 'the glamour of a remote past'. In nineteenth-century American towns where railroad and land development projects threatened to bring change, the name of Stratford conjured a sense of order, comfort, history and tradition. With Stratford, New Jersey, however, it is unclear why the town discarded its Revolutionary War identity, other than perhaps the desire for a fresh start with a new set of connotations related to 'Stratford', and the connection with British as opposed to American history.

The origins of another Stratford, in Texas, settled around 1885, involve both the U.K. destination and Stratford Hall, the Virginia home of Confederate General Robert E. Lee. Most histories attribute the Texas town name to Founder Colonel Walter Colton's interest in the American Civil War and to his English origins.[29] Additionally, Stratford, U.K. fits the proclivity for early Texan settlers to choose exotic place names – Eden, Paradise and Utopia, for example. In fact, Colton may have had both 'Stratfords' in mind when choosing this name, evoking both connections to the American Civil War and to the longer history of 'Stratford'.[30] However, the town's most recent image invokes no connections with Shakespeare, as Illustration 5.1 attests. Even though, as Sonia Massai points out, 'Shakespeare has effectively become a successful logo or brand name', to date, Stratford, Texas shows no links to Shakespeare, preferring instead 'Pheasant Capital of Texas' and 'God, Grass, and Grit' as more appealing mottoes for their town image than Shakespeare-related or American Civil War associations.[31]

On the other side of the world, Stratford, New Zealand and Stratford, Australia were also part of the boom of Global Stratfords around 1880. The New Zealand town was originally called 'Stratford-

Illustration 5.1. Stratford, Texas.

upon-Patea', named in 1877 by William Compton of the Taranaki Waste Lands Board, who 'was known to have a literary turn of mind' and saw a resemblance between the River Avon and the Patea River.[32] Sixty-seven of the town streets are named after Shakespearean characters. Stratford, Australia was founded nine years later (in 1886) in Victoria, appropriately along the Avon River.

The Later History of Stratfords

While these towns offer insight into the myriad constructions of 'Stratford' worldwide from the seventeenth century through the nineteenth, their various evolutions also allow us to chart the changing associations of Stratford with Shakespeare over the last century or so, in different times and places, and to survey the various degrees to which these spaces have invested meaning through Shakespeare. We have seen that Stratford, Texas shows no Shakespearean connections. Stratford, Iowa likewise only recently began to link their town more overtly to Shakespeare, with a new motto 'The place to be', and promotion of the Des Moines-based touring company 'Shakespeare on the Loose'.[33] The faux Tudor façade of the library on the main street (Illustration 5.2) also provides an English atmosphere to the otherwise mundane downtown.

Illustration 5.2. Stratford, Iowa Library. Photo courtesy of Ashton B. Crew.

Unfortunately, the associations with Shakespeare do not seem to have bestowed great prosperity to rural Iowa. The Chicago and Northwest Railroad once ran through the town, but no longer does, and according to the 2000 census, Stratford, Iowa had only 746 citizens.

In Stratford, New Zealand, two relatively recent tributes to Shakespeare seek to underline the town's connection with the famous poet. The most unusual tribute to Shakespeare is the town glockenspiel, which plays the balcony scene from *Romeo and Juliet* three times a day. The glockenspiel (the only one in New Zealand) is also relatively recent, completed in 1999, with figures carved by Nigel Ogle, the curator of the Tawhiti Museum of New Zealand heritage, combining Shakespeare with New Zealand nationalism.[34] Sculptor Roger Peters presented a bust of Shakespeare to the town in 1998, two years before beginning his Quaternary Institute, located in the countryside near Stratford. The Institute comprises a three-year programme which 'develop[s] a level of education commensurate with the previously unrecognized coherent and comprehensive philosophy evident in William Shakespeare's Sonnets and other works' where students 'develop a philosophic attitude consistent with the natural logic of life'.[35]

In spite of the efforts of the New Zealand Stratford Shakespeare Society and Creative New Zealand, this Stratford has yet to become a tourist destination. According to one recent guidebook, 'A glance at the street names in Stratford will soon confirm your suspicion that this rural service centre and eastern gateway to the Egmont National Park was named after Shakespeare's birthplace in England. But there the similarity really ends'. The writer attests that Stratford is 'a pleasant little town but there is little to detain you beyond a meal, a coffee, and perhaps a look at the Glockenspiel'.[36] Sculptor Roger Peters seems to have almost single-handedly developed the Shakespearean associations of Stratford in New Zealand, through his bust of Shakespeare and his sonnet-based philosophical programme, though the success of his Quaternary Institute is unclear.

Shakespearean Stratfords

Many of these Stratfords have had a tumultuous relationship with Shakespeare, with some choosing not to invoke associations with the famous writer and others experimenting with Shakespeare-themed entertainments and resonances.[37] The two Stratfords that have aligned themselves most closely with Shakespeare, through various evolving products and practices, are in Ontario and Connecticut, though with different results. The Canada Company's choice of Stratford as a name perhaps has its most serious repercussions in The Stratford Festival, founded in 1953, which now boasts 'the largest classical theatre in North America'.[38] As Margaret Groome has argued, 'for Canada, the plans for a Shakespeare Festival to be held in Stratford tapped into both a long-sought cultural respectability and desire for a national theatre. With the founding of the Stratford Festival, "culture" and the idea of a national theatre became conflated with Shakespeare'.[39] When searching for a place to establish a national theatre with an emphasis on Shakespeare, founder Tom Patterson remarked that the choice of Stratford was 'absolutely natural' because there was a ready-made 'city named Stratford, on a river named Avon. We had a beautiful park system. We had wards and schools with such names as Hamlet, Falstaff, Romeo and Juliet'.[40] By naming the town Stratford and setting up an atmosphere of Shakespeariana (through street and school names), this small town eighty miles from Toronto was ripe for the cultural development that now characterises its Shakespeare-based identity.[41]

The mayor at the time, Dave Simpson, remarked, 'I don't know anything about Shakespeare, except that it's the name of a school on the east end of town. But if it's good for Stratford, then, I'm all for it'.[42] If we take the mayor at his word, the town's incentive to develop the Festival had more to do with economics than aesthetics. In fact, Patterson hoped to use the Festival (and the Shakespeare brand) as a mode of economic revival for Stratford. As Margaret Groome points out, Patterson aimed to 'establish a festival that would do for the Canadian Stratford what the Shakespeare industry was doing for the economy of mother Stratford and Warwickshire'.[43] Had Stratford, Ontario been given another name with a 'strong English connection' but one unconnected to Shakespeare, it is doubtful that 'Canada's cultural needs' would have been addressed by a Shakespeare Festival.[44]

The Festival initially imported Englishman Tyrone Guthrie as the first director, but now it currently 'aims to set the standard for classical theatre in North America', with an annual operating budget of just under $60 million, and more than 1,000 employees. Even though the town and festival depend on the cultural authority of the Shakespeare brand, the most recent season (2019) includes only three Shakespeare plays out of twelve productions.[45] This proportion suggests that plans for the revival of the Festival Theatre in Stratford, Connecticut (discussed below), which did not predominantly include plays by Shakespeare, may not have been so misguided after all.

While the naming of Stratford, Connecticut originated with first-generation immigrants in the 1630s from Stratford in England, it is only in the last century that the town began to invest in the potential power of its connection with Shakespeare, with mixed success at best.[46] Founded in 1955, the Shakespeare Festival Theatre was modelled after the Globe, with the largest stage between New York and Boston, and hosted prominent actors including Katharine Hepburn, John Houseman, James Earl Jones, Christopher Plummer, Lynn Redgrave and Christopher Walken. In the theatre's heyday, its evocation of a Shakespearean atmosphere was initially successful: 'before or after the show, theatergoers picnicked on the lawn while gazing at the dreamy mouth of the Housatonic River as if they were sitting at Shakespeare's Stratford birthplace on the River Avon. Wandering madrigal singers entertained them and Shakespeare himself (or an actor in costume) would mingle'.[47]

Even with the impressive theatre, the proximity to New York City, the prosperity of its home state and the availability of good actors, the association with Shakespeare evidently was not enough to ensure success for this New England Stratford and its cultural life; the theatre filed for bankruptcy in 1982 and until recently remained 'derelict, its gray painted exterior flaking, its outdoor balconies sagging, its signature Elizabethan sundial fading. A gaping hole in the roof lets in rain that has weakened the backstage floor'.[48] An article in *The New York Times* lamented the fact that 'a state with one of the nation's wealthiest and most educated populations could allow a gem to rot away for a quarter century and permit a generation of Northeastern children to miss out on live Shakespeare'.[49] The answer probably has much to do with the fluctuating cultural cachet of Shakespeare, which has been a source of controversy in the many attempts to revive the theatre, and which underlines Sonia Massai's point that 'the Shakespeare industry is not immune from shifts in economic and marketing strategies'.[50]

In 2008, the Stratford, Connecticut town council selected William (Bill) Hanney, who formerly managed Theater by the Sea in Matunuck, Rhode Island, to renovate the theatre for $3.1 million. Hanney, however, attested that he had 'never seen a Shakespeare play and thinks Shakespeare is not what modern audiences crave', and thus did not plan to centre the revived theatre on Shakespeare.[51] Even though the town council approved a contract with Hanney, Mayor James R. Miron refused to sign a contract that 'does not devote a significant portion of the year' to Shakespeare.[52] In 2010, his successor Mayor John A. Harkins agreed, and also refused to sign, prompting the town council to rescind their deal with Hanney.[53]

The planned revival of the Festival Theatre in Connecticut was an uphill task, caught between its heritage as a site of Shakespeare performance, its financial need to offer 'what modern audiences crave', and other imperatives related to the economic difficulties of Southern Connecticut. According to the former mayor of Stratford and some members of the town council, Shakespeare should 'retain a starring role' comparable to his success in the sister city of Stratford, Ontario.[54] Likewise, Stratford Councilman Matt Catalano hoped to 'use a revived theater and its Shakespeare Festival and theatre revival [as] the cornerstone of economic and cultural development ... much the way Stratford sister cities and communities have around the world'.[55] Not all residents of Stratford were convinced that the town's connection to Shakespeare was the best panacea; according to a recent article, there are 'a lot of people who would like to see the theater taken down and the land used for another purpose'. In response, Arts Commissioner Ed Goodrich proclaimed that 'tearing that theater down would be like ripping the guts out of the town of Stratford. It was once its heart and soul ... and can be again'.[56]

In 2011 the Stratford Arts Commission opened the theatre to the public 'to view and reminisce', as part of a new 'Festival! Stratford'. Presumably, their intent was to promote the local memories of the theatre as a way to reinvest its Shakespearean value,[57] but a fire in January 2019 destroyed the theatre beyond repair. The identity of this New England Stratford and its tumultuous connection with Shakespeare reflect the problems of modern audiences, economics and cultural development, and sustaining the practices necessary to keep up the town's association with Shakespeare has been beyond their means, both financially and culturally, and now the theatre itself is gone.

The various imported Stratfords discussed in this chapter, from colonial America to contemporary New Zealand, suggest the complex associations between the name of 'Stratford' and its (now almost inevitable) link to Shakespeare, from evoking a sense of tradition, stability and history; to the complicated relationships between national identities. Shakespeare has not meant unequivocal success for the Stratfords which have sought to exploit the Shakespeare connections of their town name, but perhaps this is indicative of the shifting values and meanings behind both 'Stratford' and Shakespeare, from the nineteenth century to the present, and in various geographical locales and economic circumstances. Even the Stratfords that have 'inscrib[ed]' their Shakespearean associations 'in the landscape',[58] through the Stratford Festival, street and school names in Ontario, and the Festival Theatre in Connecticut – have not been able to sustain a thorough Shakespearisation; the Stratford, Ontario Festival can only give over less than one-fourth of their repertoire to Shakespeare.

In spite of this problematic history, the proclivity for associating spaces with Shakespeare is far from over: Prince Edward Island, Canada, amalgamated several communities together in 1995 to form a single 'Stratford'.[59] The global community of 'Stratford' is now linked through the 'Stratford Sister Cities' programme, but notably, such an exchange is only available for those Stratfords who 'have a connection with (or special interest in) Shakespeare'.[60] These sister Stratfords seek to invest meaning in their locales by participating in a global Shakespeare network, extending the resonance of 'Stratford' as a place well beyond its original confines of Warwickshire.[61]

Katherine Scheil is Professor of English at the University of Minnesota. She is the author of *The Taste of the Town: Shakespearian Comedy and the Early Eighteenth-Century Theatre* (2003), *She Hath Been Reading: Women and Shakespeare Clubs in America* (2012), and *Imagining Shakespeare's Wife: The Afterlife of Anne Hathaway* (2018).

Notes

1. William Winter, *Shakespeare's England* (New York: Macmillan, 1893), 79. Winter's work was published in America in two volumes (*The Trip to England* and *English Rambles*) in 1879, 1881 and 1884. His essay 'Shakespeare's Home' appeared in *Harper's Magazine* in 1879. I am grateful to Julie Sanders for her thoughtful and generous feedback on this chapter.

2. Nicola J. Watson, 'Shakespeare on the Tourist Trail', in *The Cambridge Companion to Shakespeare and Popular Culture*, ed. Robert Shaughnessy (Cambridge: Cambridge University Press, 2007), 213. Margaret Fuller Ossoli pointed out in her 1895 essay that 'the room where Shakespeare was born has been an object of devotion only for forty years'. *At Home and Abroad; or, Things and Thoughts in*

America and Europe (Boston: Roberts Brothers, 1895), 166. For an extended history of the birthplace, see Julia Thomas, *Shakespeare's Shrine: The Bard's Birthplace and the Invention of Stratford-upon-Avon* (Philadelphia: University of Pennsylvania Press, 2012).

3. A longer version of this chapter would include further discussion of portable birthplaces (such as the infamous plan by P. T. Barnum to import the Henley Street house to America) and outpost Anne Hathaway Cottages in such locales as South Dakota and Wisconsin, as part of what Kim C. Sturgess calls the 'gradual involvement of the American people in the material ownership of Shakespeare'. *Shakespeare and the American Nation* (Cambridge: Cambridge University Press, 2003), 182.

4. Tim Cresswell, *Place: A Short Introduction* (Malden, MA: Blackwell, 2004), 11.

5. Samuel Orcutt, *A History of the Old Town of Stratford and the City of Bridgeport, Connecticut*, Part 1 (Fairfield: Fairfield County Historical Society, 1886), 123–24. Descendants of the Beardsley family also settled in New York, naming their town Avon 'in honor of the old river in England'. Several towns in the U.S. have taken on the truncated name of 'Avon'. Avon, Connecticut, incorporated in 1830, seems to have been named after the river Avon rather than 'Stratford'. See http://www.town.avon.ct.us/Public_Documents/AvonCT_AvonInfo/brief_history; http://www.avonhistoricalsociety.org/HistoryofAvon.htm (last accessed 13 August 2012). Avon, Illinois was originally called Woodville, but the postmaster changed the town name to Avon in 1852, probably after Avon, New York. The township of Avon in Illinois was also named by settlers from Avon, New York, after deliberating over Hainesville and Eureka as possible names. See Edward Callary, *Place Names of Illinois* (Urbana: University of Illinois Press, 2009), 20. See also Florence Fennessy and Grace Woods, *Centennial History of Avon* (Avon: Avon Sentinel, 1937), 2–3; Diana Dretske, *What's in a Name? The Origin of Place names in Lake County, Illinois* (Wauconda, IL: Lake County Discovery Museum, 2002).

6. *A Banquet of Jeasts, or Change of Cheare* (London, 1630), no. 259, cited in *The Shakspere Allusion-Book*, I:347. As Nicola J. Watson points out, it was not until the eighteenth century when 'the first stirrings of the Stratford tourist industry as we know and love it today' became evident (199).

7. Roger Pringle, 'The Rise of Stratford as Shakespeare's Town', *The History of an English Borough: Stratford-Upon-Avon, 1196–1996*, ed. Robert Bearman (Stroud, Gloucestershire: Sutton Publishing, 1997), 161.

8. According to one history of Stratford, NH, the first tree was cut down by Isaac Johnson and Archippas Blogget, who 'tried which could cut his tree down first, and Johnson succeeded'. Both were from Stratford, CT. See Samuel Orcutt, *A History of the Old Town of Stratford and the City of Bridgeport, Connecticut*, Part II (Fairfield: Fairfield County Historical Society, 1886), 1108.

9. Pringle, 163.

10. Washington Irving, 'Stratford-on-Avon', from *The Sketch Book of Geoffrey Crayon, Gent.*, 2 vols. (London, 1820), in *Americans on Shakespeare, 1776–1914*, ed. Peter Rawlings (Aldershot: Ashgate, 1999), 43. When Nathaniel Hawthorne visited Stratford in 1855, he similarly described the birthplace as 'woefully shabby and dingy, coarsely built, and such as the most poetical imagination would find it difficult to idealize'. 'Recollections of a Gifted Woman', *Atlantic Monthly* 11 (1863), in Rawlings, 220.

11. Sturgess, 129. When P. T. Barnum visited Stratford in 1844, he was given Irving's 'Sketch Book' as a guide. See P. T. Barnum, *Struggles and Triumphs: or, Forty years' Recollections* (Hartford: J. B. Burr, 1870), 231–32. Roger Pringle remarks that Irving's book 'did much to ensure a steadily increasing patronage of the town by visitors from both the old world and the new' (167).

12. Carolynn Bart-Riedstra and Lutzen Riedstra, *Stratford: Its Heritage and Its Festival* (Toronto: James Lorimer and Company, 1999), 18.

13. Alan Rayburn, 'The Shakespearean Connection', *Canadian Geographic* 115, 1 (January/February 1995), 77. Rayburn discusses other Canadian locales with Shakespeare names including Shakespeare Township, Hamlet Township and Macbeth Township in Ontario; Mount Iago, Mount Benvolio and Mount Macbeth in British Columbia; Mount Juliet and Mount Romeo on Vancouver Island; Lakes Timon and Yorick in Quebec; the Nerissa post office in Nova Scotia; and the towns of Oberon and Portia in Manitoba. It would be interesting to know (though difficult to research) how local citizens see their Stratfordian/Shakespearean identities.

14. Rayburn, 77.

15. Kim Sturgess points out that the advertisement for the previous sale of the Birthplace in 1805 'did not mention Shakespeare or any historic associations' (183). See Watson and Sturgess for discussions of the development of Stratford as a tourist destination.

16. Sturgess, 130–31.

17. Rawlings, 14.

18. Effie R. Knapp, 'History of the Eugene Shakespeare Club', MS 227, Special Collections and University Archives, University of Oregon Library.

19. This might lend support to Michael Dobson's argument that 'the very existence of a Shakespeare industry on [the American] side of the Atlantic may be a sign of the ultimate failure of the American revolution'. 'Fairly Brave New World: Shakespeare, the American Colonies, and the American Revolution', *Renaissance Drama* 23 (1992), 189.

20. I have not been able to find any information about the history of Stratford, Pennsylvania, which suggests that the practices necessary to maintain a Shakespearean identity are either dormant or never existed here in the first place.

21. Péter Dávidházi, *The Romantic Cult of Shakespeare: Literary Reception in Anthropological Perspective* (New York: St. Martin's Press, 1998), 34–107.

22. David Thelen, 'Memory and American History', *The Journal of American History* 75, 4 (1989), 1125.

23. Rawlings, 316. Similarly, Washington Irving described the cottage of the sexton of Holy Trinity Church as 'a picture of that neatness, order, and comfort, which pervade all the humblest dwellings in this country'. Rawlings, 45.

24. Samuel Schoenbaum, *Shakespeare's Lives* (Oxford: Clarendon, 1970), 690. This also relates to Eric Hobsbawm's observation that 'the contrast between the constant change in innovation of the modern world and the attempt to structure at least some parts of social life within it as unchanging and invariant ... makes the "invention of tradition" so interesting'. 'Introduction: Inventing Traditions', in *The Invention of Tradition*, ed. Eric Hobsbawm and Terence Ranger (Cambridge: Cambridge University Press, 1983), 2. Harriet Beecher Stowe's 1854 description of Shakespeare's birthplace evokes just such a rendition; she remarks that 'the materials out of which [Shakespeare's] mind was woven were dyed in the grain,

in the haunted springs of tradition'. Harriet Beecher Stowe, *Sunny Memories of Foreign Lands*, vol. 1 (Boston: Phillips, Sampson, and Company, 1854), 195. The complexities of the Iowan appropriation of 'Stratford' speak to John J. Joughin's point that 'Shakespeare has often been co-opted to secure nationalism' but has also 'continued to contest and transform it in complex and contradictory ways'. *Shakespeare and National Culture* (Manchester: Manchester University Press, 1997), 1–2.

25. Rawlings, 215.

26. We might also see the adoption of 'Stratford' and its connotations as an example of what Thomas Cartelli calls 'an American shortcut to greatness' through appropriation of Shakespeare. *Repositioning Shakespeare: National Formations, Postcolonial Appropriations* (London: Routledge, 1999), 32. In his well-known unofficial guidebook to Stratford, Washington Irving reflected on Shakespeare's ability to 'spread the magic of his mind over the very face of nature; to give to things and places a charm and character not their own, and to turn this "working-day world" into a perfect fairy land'. Rawlings, 56.

27. For Shakespeare in the American West, see Levette J. Davidson, 'Shakespeare in the Rockies', *Shakespeare Quarterly* 4 (1953): 39–49 and Richard Van Orman, 'The Bard in the West', *The Western Historical Quarterly* 5 (1974): 29–38.

28. http://www.stratfordnj.org/borough-history.html (last accessed 24 April 2019).

29. According to one source of Texas place-names, 'If it can be believed that Colonel Walter Colton, an early settler, paid homage to Stratford-on-Avon, birthplace of Shakespeare, then this Texas community is Stratford-on-Coldwater-Creek. A more likely influence, however, is Colonel Colton's admiration for General Robert E. Lee and his decision to honor Lee's birthplace at Stratford, Virginia. The colonel owned the townsite when the railroad came'. Fred Tarpley, *1001 Texas Place Names* (Austin: University of Texas Press, 1980), 193. One source attests that Stratford was 'named by Englishman Walter Colton for Stratford-on-Avon, birthplace of William Shakespeare. Another story says that Colton named Stratford after Stratford, Virginia, birthplace of Robert E. Lee'. Mavis P. Kelsey, Sr., and Donald H. Dyal, *The Courthouses of Texas* (College Station: Texas A&M Press, 1993), 241.

30. See Al Lowman, 'From Eden to Uncertain: Observations on People and Place Names in Texas', in *Texas Country: The Changing Rural Scene*, ed. Glen E. Lich and Dona B. Reeves-Marquardt (College Station: Texas A&M Press, 1986): 37–65 (esp. 54–55). There is also a town named Iago, Texas.

31. Sonia Massai, 'Defining Local Shakespeares', in *World-Wide Shakespeares: Local Appropriations in Film and Performance* (London: Routledge, 2005), 4.

32. http://www.waymarking.com/waymarks/WM5XVK_Shakespeare_Bust_Stratford_Taranaki_New_Zealand (last accessed 24 April 2019).

33. In her history of Stratford covering over 100 years, Hannah Nelson includes almost no references to Shakespeare associations. *An Era in the History of Stratford, Iowa and Community, 1840–1960* (Stratford, Iowa: Stratford Promotions Committee, 2005).

34. http://www.waymarking.com/waymarks/WM6BXB_Glockenspiel_Stratford_Taranaki_New_Zealand (last accessed 24 April 2019). This nationalistic mélange supports John J. Joughin's argument that 'Shakespeare has become the national poet of a variety of countries in particular forms' (1).

35. http://www.quaternaryinstitute.com (last accessed 24 April 2019).

36. Darroch Donald, *Footprint New Zealand* (Bath: Footprint, 2003), 333.

37. As Tim Cresswell points out, places are 'never finished' and are 'constantly being performed', so these efforts to sustain a relationship with Shakespeare require consistent maintenance (37).

38. Irena R. Makaryk, 'Introduction', in *Shakespeare in Canada: 'A World Elsewhere'?*, ed. Diana Brydon and Irena R. Makaryk (Toronto: University of Toronto Press, 2002), 23.

39. Margaret Groome, 'Stratford and the Aspirations for a Canadian National Theatre', in *Shakespeare in Canada,* 109.

40. Tom Patterson and Allan Gould, *First Stage: The Making of the Stratford Festival* (Willowdale, ON: Firefly, 1999), 26.

41. See Groome for discussion of the issues of a Shakespeare-based national theatre in relation to ideas of Canadian nationalism.

42. Patterson and Gould, 34.

43. Groome, 123.

44. Groome, 108.

45. https://www.stratfordfestival.ca/WhatsOn/ThePlays (last accessed 17 January 2019).

46. See Cresswell, 12 and 98 for discussion of power and space.

47. Joseph Berger, 'Aye, There's the Rub: Would the Bard Pay?', *The New York Times,* 10 August 2008.

48. Ibid.

49. Ibid.

50. Massai, 4. Diana E. Henderson has argued that Shakespeare has 'been an idea and an institution – though the content of what he/it signified has been as changeable as performance itself'. 'Shakespeare: The Theme Park', in *Shakespeare After Mass Media,* ed. Richard Burt (New York: Palgrave, 2002), 107–126 (111).

51. Berger, 'Aye, There's the Rub'.

52. Ibid.

53. Richard Weizel, 'Curtains for Yet Anther Bid to Revive Shakespeare Theater', *Connecticut Post* 9 February 2010.

54. Berger, 'Aye, There's the Rub'.

55. Richard Weizel, 'Last Act for Shakespeare Theater Revival Efforts?', *Connecticut Post,* 28 February 2010.

56. Ibid.

57. http://www.festivalstratford.org (last accessed 24 April 2019).

58. Cresswell, 85.

59. William B. Hamilton, *Place Names of Atlantic Canada* (Toronto: University of Toronto Press, 1996), 33.

60. The Stratford Sister Cities programme began in the 1980s and includes Stratfords in the U.K., Ontario, Prince Edward Island, New Zealand, Australia and Connecticut. See http://stratford.org.au (last accessed 13 August).

61. We might see these practices as creating what Tim Cresswell calls a 'homogenized global space' centred on Shakespeare, where local culture is subservient to global economic forces (8). See also Susan Bennett, 'Universal Experience – The City as Tourist Stage', in *The Cambridge Companion to Performance Studies* (Cambridge: Cambridge University Press, 2008), 76–90.

Afterword

'Dear Shakespeare-land'

Investing in Stratford

Nicola J. Watson

I take my title from a letter written by the popular novelist Marie Corelli which describes her long-meditated choice in 1899 of Stratford-upon-Avon as her home.[1] The tribute is apposite because I am writing in the garden-folly set in the garden of the house she leased and eventually bought, Mason Croft, now the home of the Shake-speare Institute. Corelli must have found Mason Croft's handsome mid-eighteenth-century frontage and garden, ornamented with a free-standing classical arch in stone, not only dispiritingly dilapi-dated but dispiritingly modern, for she set about bringing it back 'to look something like it must have been in the fifteenth century', equipping the house with quantities of oak panelling and casement windows. She gave full rein to this Elizabethanising impulse in reno-vating the eighteenth-century folly as a summer study, which she liked to think of as an 'Elizabethan watch-tower', erected to look over an old farmhouse supposedly built by 'Rychard Mason'.[2] As such,

Notes for this section begin on page 98.

it would become part of her public mythos.[3] Lavishly ornamented with diamond panes of leaded glass in the windows, dark oak panelling and cabinet bookcases punctured with cut-outs of hearts, vine-covered and picturesque, the total effect is sweet, pretentious, aggressive and sentimental. Even as it re-inflects it, it is eloquent of a then century-old desire to retrieve, reconstruct and evoke Stratford's essential Elizabethanness, a desire which can be traced back all the way to the engraving of an imagined New Place inserted in Samuel Ireland's *Picturesque Views on the Upper or Warwickshire Avon* (1795). Corelli's tower therefore serves as a fitting emblem for this volume, as one among many instances of the long history of investing in Stratford to make it more 'Shakespearean'.

This Stratford has been produced in defiance of Shakespeare's own near-silence about his home town and its environs, coupled with the relative scantiness of the biographical record. It has emerged out of successive acts of imagination exerted in the first instance upon the biographical record, supplemented by judicious extraction from the Works, acts which date back to the 1760s. Site-specific acts of commemoration, memorial rituals, practices and performances associated with anniversaries, representation in the visual arts and in fiction, reiteration in the shape of replicas in other places – all these have played their part, and some of this is detailed in the important body of work by a succession of scholars on both the historical and the contemporary meanings of Stratford as 'Shakespeare's town' – work by Ivor Brown and George Fearon, Roger Pringle, Graham Holderness, Barbara Hodgdon, Diana Henderson, Douglas Lanier, Gail Marshall, Richard Schoch, and Julia Thomas.[4] Yet the history of the idea of Stratford, how it developed through successive adaptation and memorialisation, and how and in what forms it has been represented in print and visual media, has still not been written; nor do we have a full history of what interests the idea of Stratford has successively served and how this has changed or been contested. A complete account would encompass site-specific markers and their histories; site-specific memorial practices, especially the Birthday procession; depictions in travel-writing, fiction, verse, biography, drama, art, television and film; relics and souvenirs; and a sense of how 'Stratford' also comprises its environs, including Charlecote, Kenilworth, Bidford, Snitterfield and so forth. This volume starts on this task. The scope of this brief tailpiece is necessarily modest: I try to identify as yet unspoken commonalities and connections between the essays, and I explore to what extent the ways of imagining Stratford detailed here are still alive today, and what new constructions may be emerging.

I

Although locals have long benefitted from the tourist trade, the making of Stratford into 'Shakespeare's town' has mostly been the work of outsiders like Corelli.[5] From Garrick onwards, they have celebrated, defended and curated Stratford as a metropolitan, national, imperial, European, pan-Anglophone and latterly, a global resource. It has not been easy to render the universal local or the local universal, even given the useful biographical connection between the two that Shakespeare traced when he left the home of his childhood and youth for London, world metropolis, and then came back to a well-heeled retirement and a well-marked grave. There have been tensions, for example, between the rival claims of provincial home and metropolitan theatre ever since the late eighteenth century. Garrick's forced choice of Stratford as the place in which to stage his Jubilee was fateful. It required him to play up what we would now recognise as specifically romantic claims for the nature of genius as emanating from a particular, national landscape, rather than focusing on the record of the career professional working in the metropolitan theatre. The Jubilee effectively conceived Stratford as an anti-theatre within which to celebrate Shakespeare's works; the Birthday procession populated Stratford with Shakespeare's characters liberated from the stage into the place which had supposedly inspired them, affirming their link with Shakespeare's native soil rather than with show business.

The tensions, first sketched out in the Jubilee,[6] between depicting 'Shakespeare' as a native genius and conceiving 'Shakespeare' as a body of works designed to be played in the theatre, have had special force around the many and various efforts to build playhouses in Stratford. As Christy Desmet notes of the establishment of the first Memorial Theatre in 1879, 'the town's suitability as the national home for a theatre devoted to Shakespeare was hotly debated in the press' (Desmet, 6). It was felt to be inappropriately local for a national celebration – a sentiment that echoed the argument a century before over whether the Jubilee should best be celebrated in London or in Stratford. By the 1870s, however, 100 years of literary tourism had ensured that Stratford had the same or greater imaginative power as the metropolitan Pantheon, as Helen Faucit's comments on the power of the locality to add value to the theatre suggest (Desmet, 16). Thus the event combined celebration of locality (in the shape of the predictably rained-off outdoor festivities and of the local amateur actors cast in *Much Ado*) with a celebration of the metropolitan (in the shape of the professional cast and the drop curtain that identified the Memorial Theatre as a latter-day Globe). Indeed, most of the theatres built on this iconic site of 'the banks of the Avon' from Garrick's Rotunda to the Royal Shakespeare Company's (RSC's) new outdoor venue 'The Dell', have been acutely conscious of the import of their setting. The current fire-tower-like structure on the rebuilt Memorial Theatre must be unique in allowing tourists and theatre-goers to gaze out over the surrounding countryside.

The tensions between Stratford and London have also structured fiction from *Master Skylark* onwards. As Susanne Greenhalgh notes, Stratford has typically been depicted as the home from which the boy departs into the all-male adult world of the urban theatre. Although fiction has offered girls and women, including Corelli, imaginative access to the Bard through the Victorian cult of the Stratford houses of Shakespeare's sweetheart and mother, even recent fiction makes it clear that girls, and the women they grow into, stay in Stratford, as Susanne Greenhalgh shows. This trajectory from feminised domesticity towards male professionalism also structures the memoir by Shakespearean director Dominic Dromgoole, *Will and Me* (2006). Shakespeare himself, says Dromgoole, experienced the tension between 'the home and the away, the domestic and the wild, the bourgeois gent and the libertine, Stratford and London...'[7] He proposes to resolve these tensions by walking from Shakespeare's grave at Stratford to the replica Globe in London, of which he had just become artistic director. Dromgoole's imagined retracing of Shakespeare's footsteps amounts to a reading of Shakespeare's biography, in which, as Julie Sanders argues, Stratford represents domesticity, family and heterosexuality, while London represents masculine adventure and the homoerotic (Sanders, 49). In this respect, Dromgoole as Shakespeare's blokeish double is clearly a modern Master Skylark all grown up.

If Londoners from Garrick to Dromgoole have put their mark on Stratford, enthusiasts from further afield have been responsible for the some of the more expensive interventions within the town. Stratford was not initially put on the tourist map by American visitors and writers, but it has nevertheless suited them to think so, and it is certainly true that their continuing vigorous interest has done much to shape Stratford as a tourist destination. Ever since Washington Irving wrote as Geoffrey Crayon about his visit to Stratford in the 1820s, American writers have consistently depicted the American tourist as more knowledgeable and more reverential (when appropriate) than any native. Such a depiction usefully gave a special prominence and privilege to the American visitor; it seems only appropriate that American visitors were typically as keen on seeing Washington Irving's chair and poker (displayed at the inn at which he had stayed, The Red Horse) as seeing 'Shakespeare's chair' itself, housed in the Birthplace.[8] Nor did American relations with Stratford stop at tourism; as Clara Calvo notes, in the last years of the nineteenth century, American money poured in to Stratford (Calvo, 56). American desire to appropriate Shakespeare, parodically represented by Barnum's plan to buy the Birthplace in 1847 and tour it around the States, was in practice realised by conspicuous investment into Stratford.[9] This began to appear as early as 1879 with the establishment of the first Memorial Theatre, which was partially funded by American contributions. It was not coincidental that the opening ceremony featured an American, a resident and fundraiser, Kate Field (Desmet, 10).[10] Donated by George Childs in 1887, the Shakespeare Memorial Fountain and Clock Tower helpfully makes explicit the sentiments lying behind the money. American technology (a clock, a thermometer, a barometer, four weathervanes) dwarfs the slightly perfunctory British fairies, as the inspirational water of the Avon is redirected by American philanthropy into a useful drinking fountain for men, cattle, horses, and sheep, and the folk mythos of Shakespeare as a hard-drinking man is refuted by a Bard co-opted into the Temperance movement in lines from *Timon of Athens* – 'Honest water, that ne'er left man i' th' mire'. *Henry VIII* is made to prophesy something very like American-style democracy: 'In her days, every man shall eat in safety / Under his own vine, what he plants ... and those about her / From her shall read the perfect ways of honour, / And by those claim their greatness, not by blood.' (5:4, 33–38)

The Fountain commemorated Victoria's Jubilee and Shakespeare more generally, but its installation was timed to coincide with another important anniversary, the 'Centennial Year of American Independence'.[11] The dedication ceremony included the reading of a letter by James Russell Lowell, then one of America's most prominent poets, which made explicit a commonplace that activated many congruent acts of American literary memorialisation within Britain at this time:

> The possessions of the American in England are laid down on no map, yet he holds them of memory and imagination by a title such as no conquest ever established and no revolution can ever overthrow. The dust that is sacred to you is sacred to him. The annals which Shakespeare makes walk before us in flesh and blood are his no less than yours.[12]

Such claims to cultural possession are also encoded in subsequent American interventions in Stratford – the 'American window' eventually installed in Holy Trinity Church, the purchase of Harvard House, the window installed in the Guildhall Chapel, and contributions to the building of the second and third Memorial Theatres in 1926 and 1932, and the Swan in 1986. As Calvo has shown, the ideological advantages of asserting cultural possession and continuity outweighed the inconvenient historical truth that New England was explicitly built from political and religious rupture with the birthplace of the 'English speaking race' (Calvo, 67).

For those American citizens who could not afford to build a memorial in Stratford itself, there remained the option suggested by Barnum's business-plan, to transplant Stratford. As Katherine Scheil has shown, the practice of naming North American towns and cities after Stratford was widespread, and carried an equally wide range of cultural meanings; even more literal-minded was the practice of building replica Shakespeare properties and planting 'Shakespeare gardens', mostly in defiance of inhospitable climates, right around the world, a practice that peaked in America around the 1930s. This enterprise finds an echo and a commentary in Angela Carter's fantasia *Wise Children* (1991), which tells of the Chance twins and their efforts to import Stratford earth (packed in a ceramic head of Shakespeare) onto the Hollywood film-set of *A Midsummer Night's Dream*. In this fiction, Stratford, as Calvo points out, doesn't travel well; although it is reverently enshrined by the Mexican help who mistakes it for a religious relic, the soil has been used by a film-star's pet Persian cat in default of a litter-tray on the long rail journey across the continent. The Chance sisters replace the soil from the most authentic available, dug out of a facsimile Shakespearean knot-garden at a motel called the Forest of Arden, which contains a replica of Anne Hathaway's Cottage: 'Warwickshire apple-trees, imported oaks, you name it.'[13] Sprinkled onto the set by Melchior Hazard, proponent of global Shakespeare, the ersatz soil cannot save the *Dream* from being a turkey.

II

As the chapters in this volume have cumulatively shown, the time-lessness of Stratford has been continually reconstructed to accord with multiple and changing cultural investments. It is possible not just to trace the history of past investments, but the progressive era-sure of dilapidated past self-representations in favour of new ones. How many visitors nowadays could understand the neo-classical sculpture salvaged from the London frontage of Boydell's gallery, now half-concealed at the bottom of the Great Garden, as a depiction of Shakespeare torn between the muses of painting and the thea-tre? The American Fountain has lost much of its rhetorical point now that the water-troughs have been turned into planters. How many American visitors, glancing round Holy Trinity Church, notice the American window and feel, as Calvo puts it, that it provides 'a new reason for American visitors to visit Shakespeare's church'? (Calvo, 67). Does anyone notice the plaque celebrating Shakespeare the drinker on the wall of the Windmill Inn, put up in the days of neo-Elizabethan joviality that followed the present queen's corona-tion? Nonetheless, after some twenty-five years of visiting Stratford at intervals, a good deal seems much the same as it ever was. Visitors still dutifully make their way to Holy Trinity Church, around all five of the Shakespeare properties, and presumably some of them notice the many statues, plaques, street-names, murals and so forth that reference the Bard. Many of the organised experiences that Stratford offers remain fundamentally Victorian in their emphasis on biogra-phy and the outdoorsy merriness of Old England. The RSC offers 'The Walk: Shakespeare's Life in Stratford', for example, which sup-posedly 'brings Shakespeare back to life'. Events and activities for 2011 promised 'Spring Merriment', a 'traditional May Day', and the 'Sheep Shearers' Feast'. All of this remains susceptible to Douglas Lanier's reading of Stratford as 'a symbolic alternative to – and thus potentially a critique of – the alienation and fragmentation character-istic of postmodern life.'[14] Less readily assimilable to Lanier's view, of course, is the continued presence of commercial Shakespearean kitsch: the guesthouse, hostelrie, tea-shop, giftshop, and wedding business operating under undecidably sincere or jokey names inspired by the Bard still springs up, and let's not even start on the problem of souvenirs.

Yet I think there are recognisably new stories developing in Stratford. The present astonishing proliferation of theatres – the newly redesigned Memorial Theatre, the Swan, the Courtyard and the RSC's new outdoor professional venue, The Dell – is matched by the current emphasis within the Shakespeare properties on describing Stratford as theatrically inspirational for everyone, a locus for the visionary, the fantastic and the magical. The association of Shakespeare with magic and the supernatural is not in itself new; it dates back to the early nineteenth century, which was fond of imagining Shakespeare lolling about on the banks of the Avon haloed by clouds of fairies out of *A Midsummer Night's Dream*. Still, in 2012, what one might call the 'magicness' of Shakespeare was being promoted with new intensity. There was a new insistence on putting Shakespeare's words into locations, which argued at one and the same time that Shakespeare's words 'naturally' emanated from place, and that his words generated the meaning of place. Thus, at each property, there was a new emphasis on the genesis and power of imaginative writing, on that writing realised in theatrical performance, and on visitor participation. The traditional lure of getting 'closer to Shakespeare' was now supplemented at the Birthplace with a promise that you could be 'part of the performance': 'Actors bring to life your favourite Shakespeare characters throughout the Birthplace and gardens. ... Our actors may even invite you to play alongside them.'[15] Mary Arden's house now celebrated childlike play as the ground of genius; here you were invited to write out some of Shakespeare's lines with a quill pen, or dress up in costumes piled higgledy-piggledy in an RSC costume hamper. In Anne Hathaway's Cottage, 'the most romantic of all the houses', visitors are encouraged into a 'willow cabin where you can listen to Shakespeare's sonnets read by famous actors'. If you ventured beyond the domestic idyll of the cottage garden and traditional orchard, you came upon a new 'woodland walk', the winding paths of which were hung with snippets of text, figures of fairies and masks, floating above head-height, evoking a mish-mash of different plays. This installation went well beyond the established traditions of showing the Hathaway house as a place of springtime courtship. It simultaneously made it into the ground of Shakespeare's inspiration and a site dramatising collective memory of Shakespeare's language.

Hall's Croft was now eerily populated by dummies wearing costumes from the plays. Nash's house displayed extraordinary everyday objects from the Birthplace Trust collections, 'curated' by Macbeth, Romeo and other characters, on appropriate themes such as 'sleep' or 'love' in such a way that the objects seemed to exhale a vapour of quotations from each play. Outside, the Great Garden was filled with sculptures that depict figures from the plays coming into being, as though the whole garden were instinct with Shakespearean creation and his own memory of it. 'Stand at the place where we believe Shakespeare wrote some of his later works, including *The Tempest*', urges the flyer. The deliberated magic-ness is underscored by the playful topiary that morphs a bush into a bear and thence into the unspoken line from *A Midsummer Night's Dream:* 'How easy is a bush supposed a bear' (5: 1, 22). The old desire for contact with the historical, 'authentic' Shakespeare, the biographical drive to 'explain' Shakespeare by Stratford, were being displaced by the experiential hypothesis that the places in which Shakespeare was inspired will bring out the Shakespearean in you, too.

What would it be to have the Shakespearean brought out in you? The Birthplace digital initiative, 'Living Shakespeare: Documenting the Stories of Pilgrimage to Shakespeare's Home', (http://livingshakespeare.com, launched April 2011), which posted video interviews with visitors from all around the world, included an interview with one Nicole from Cambridge, MA who displays Shakespeare's signature tattooed on her stomach. This insistence on consuming Shakespeare as an intimately personal experience was itself not new, but it sat oddly with the contemporaneous efforts by the Birthplace entrance exhibit to promote Shakespeare's global legacy. The incongruity prompted me to agree with Graham Holderness[16] that a revaluation of past readings of the Stratford experience was now due. However, there was not much evidence on the ground for Holderness's contention that out of Shakespeare's Stratford there might develop a new formulation of Englishness. My sense, on the contrary, was that the national was vanishing into the individual on the one hand, and being erased by the global on the other. To my mind, Stratford showed signs of becoming more of what Julian Barnes describes in *England, England*, more of 'a magical event' (cited by Holderness, 218–19). This sounds perilously close to advertising copy for Disneyland, but it had its precedent in the Shakespeare canon.[17] It could be said that in *A Midsummer Night's Dream* Shakespeare had already written the script for tourist Stratford's guiding vision. This is, after all, a play which bridges the long-standing tensions that I have been describing as constitutive of the town's identity: the amateur and the professional, the countryside and the city, the land and the theatre.

The claim to magic-ness in 2012 could surface as banal, feminised frippery – Henley Street, for instance, a shop that celebrated the perpetual magic of Christmas but a shop dedicated to a multitude of fairies and witches. Or it could surface in an aggressively masculine register, part sub-Ted Hughes and part sub-D. H. Lawrence, as it does in Dromgoole's memoir: 'This was the reality Shakespeare came from, a physical world of dirt in the fingernails, milk on the lips, and still-born sheep left in the fields for pigs to munch on; and an imaginary world, rich with primitive superstitions, as real as the carrots they dug up.'[18] Yet the idea of magical transformation retains comedic and healing potential. And indeed, since 2012, Stratford has become ever more akin to the fabric of a dream, increasingly reformulating itself as a reservoir of creativity. Such is the statement made by the 2016 redevelopment of New Place to a design by Tim O'Brien. This garden celebrates the romantic blast of Shakespearean genius that silently, perpetually blows across Shakespeare's chair, in which visitors are invited to sit and take their selfies.

Nicola J. Watson has taught at Oxford, Harvard, and Northwestern, and presently holds a chair at the Open University. She has published three monographs, ranging in subject from the fiction of the romantic period, through to the cultural after-lives of Elizabeth I, and, most recently, the history of literary tourism in *The Literary Tourist: Readers and Places in Romantic and Victorian Britain* (Palgrave, 2006). She is also the editor of a collection of essays, *Literary Tourism and Nineteenth-Century Culture* (Palgrave, 2009). Her essays dedicated to Shakespeare's cultural after-lives have included 'Shakespeare on the Tourist Trail' for the *Cambridge Companion to Shakespeare and Popular Culture*, an essay on Sir Walter Scott's effect on the reception of Shakespeare for the series *Great Shakespeareans*, and 'Gardening with Shakespeare' in Calvo and Kahn eds. *Celebrating Shakespeare: Commemoration and Cultural Memory* (CUP, 2016). Her latest monograph, *The Author's Effects: On the Writer's House Museum* is forthcoming from OUP in 2019.

Notes

All references to the plays are from Stanley Wells and Gary Taylor, *William Shakespeare: The Complete Works* 2nd edn. (Oxford: Clarendon Press, 2005).

1. See Stanley Wells, 'Foreword', in *Catalogue of an exhibition of books, manuscripts, letters, photographs and other items relating to Marie Corelli: in her former home, Mason Croft, Stratford-upon-Avon...9 June-3 July, 1964* (Stratford-upon-Avon: The Shakespeare Institute, University of Birmingham, 1964); Teresa Ransom, *The Mysterious Miss Marie Corelli: Queen of Victorian Best-Sellers* (Stroud: Sutton, 1999), 98.

2. Thomas F. G. Coates and R. S. Warren Bell, *Marie Corelli: The Writer and the Woman* (London: Hutchinson, 1903), 319. For a contemporaneous photograph, see Coates and Bell, plate facing page 312; on the history of the folly itself, see Maureen Bell, 'A brief history of Mason Croft', www.birmingham.ac.uk/schools/edacs/departments/shakespeare/about/mason-croft-history.aspx (last accessed 29 Aug 2012).

3. Coates and Bell tellingly provide a view from the 'watch-tower' through the classical arch as their frontispiece. It is generally accepted that Corelli was the original for E. F. Benson's fictional character 'Lucia' who begins her career by filling her house with all things 'Elizabethan' and designing a Shakespeare spring garden which she calls 'Perdita's garden'.

4. See Ivor Brown and George Fearon, *Amazing Monument: A Short History of the Shakespeare Industry* (London: William Heinemann, 1939); Graham Holderness, 'Bardolatry: The cultural materialist's guide to Stratford-upon-Avon', in *The Shakespeare Myth*, ed. Graham Holderness (Manchester: Manchester University Press, 1988), 2–15; Roger Pringle, 'The Rise of Stratford as Shakespeare's Town', in *The History of an English Borough: Stratford-upon-Avon, 1196–1996*, ed. Robert Bearman (Stroud: Sutton Publishing, 1997); Barbara Hodgdon, 'Stratford's Empire of Shakespeare; or, Fantasies of Origin, Authorship, and Authenticity: The Museum and the Souvenir', in *The Shakespeare Trade: Performances and Appropriations*, ed. Barbara Hodgdon (Philadelphia: University of Pennsylvania Press, 1998); Diana E. Henderson, 'Shakespeare: The Theme Park', in *Shakespeare After Mass Media*, ed. Richard Burt (New York: Palgrave, 2002); Douglas Lanier, *Shakespeare and Modern Popular Culture* (Oxford: Oxford University Press, 2002); Gail Marshall, 'Women Re-read Shakespeare Country', in *Literary Tourism and Nineteenth-century Culture*, ed. Nicola J. Watson (Basingstoke: Palgrave Macmillan, 2009), 95–105; Julia Thomas, 'Bringing down the House: Restoring the Birthplace', in *Literary Tourism and Nineteenth-century Culture*, ed. Nicola J. Watson (Basingstoke: Palgrave Macmillan, 2009), 73–83; Richard Schoch, 'The Birth of Shakespeare's Birthplace', *Theatre Survey* 53.2 (Sept 2012), 181–201.

5. Of course, for those less interested in Shakespeare than the average creative writer or humanities academic, Stratford is like any other historic English market town: despite the best efforts of the Royal Shakespeare Company and the Shakespeare Birthplace Trust, most visitors come to shop and eat, and fewer than 15 per cent of them visit either the theatres or any of the Shakespeare properties.

6. For a detailed account of the Jubilee, see Christian Deelman, *The Great Shakespeare Jubilee* (London: Michael Joseph, 1964).

7. Dominick Dromgoole, *Will and Me: How Shakespeare Took Over My Life* (London: Allen Lane, 2006), 218.

8. See Nicola J. Watson, *The Literary Tourist: Readers and Places in Romantic and Victorian Britain* (Basingstoke: Palgrave Macmillan, 2006) and 'Shakespeare on the Tourist Trail', in *The Cambridge Companion to Shakespeare and Popular Culture*, ed. Robert Shaughnessy (Cambridge: Cambridge University Press, 2007), 199–226.

9. See Kim Sturgess, *Shakespeare and the American Nation* (Cambridge: Cambridge University Press, 2004), 181–84 for some discussion of this well-known story, deriving ultimately from Barnum's autobiographical memoir.

10. Ibid., 181–82, 187.

11. L. Clarke Davis, *Story of the Memorial Fountain to Shakespeare at Stratford-upon-Avon* (1890) (USA: Kessinger Publishing, 2003), 27.

12. Quoted in Davis, 37.

13. Angela Carter, *Wise Children* (London: Chatto and Windus, 1991), 121.

14. Lanier, 145.

15. Ann Donnelly and Elizabeth Woledge, *Shakespeare: Work, Life and Times,* Official Guide, (Stratford: Shakespeare Birthplace Trust, 2011).

16. Graham Holderness, 'Shakespeare-land', in *This England, That Shakespeare*, ed. Willy Maley and Margaret Tudeau-Clayton (Aldershot: Ashgate, 2010), 201–20.

17. See Henderson, *passim*, for a less sanguine view.

18. Dromgoole, 228.

Index

NOTE: Page references with an *f* are figures; page references with an n will be found in Notes.